Sizzling Chops & Devilish Spins

Sizzling Chops & Devilish Spins

PING-PONG
AND THE ART OF
STAYING ALIVE

Jerome Charyn

This book is for Marty Reisman,
Dick Miles, and Jean-Louis Fleury

And Tim Boggan

Copyright © 2001 Jerome Charyn

Published in the United States by
Four Walls Eight Windows
39 West 14th Street
New York, NY 10011
http://www.fourwallseightwindows.com

UK offices:
Four Walls Eight Windows / Turnaround
Unit 3 Olympia Trading Estate
Coburg Road, Wood Green
London N22 6TZ

First printing October 2001.

Library of Congress Cataloging-in-Publication Data:
Charyn, Jerome
   Sizzling chops and devilish spins : ping-pong and the art of staying alive.
      p. cm.
   Includes bibliographical references.
   ISBN 1-56858-207-2 (alk. paper)
    1. Table tennis--History--Anecdotes. 2. Charyn, Jerome. I. Title.

GV1005.15 .C53 2001
796.34'6--dc21

                          2001033662

Cover and interior design / typesetting: A. Galperin

The photograph on page 94 appears courtesy of Malcolm Anderson. All
other photographs used through the courtesy of Marty Reisman, Dick Miles,
Tim Boggan, and the author.

Printed in the United States

10 9 8 7 6 5 4 3 2 1

Contents

Acknowledgments

FEW SPORTS HAVE BEEN LUCKY enough to have a full-time chronicler like Tim Boggan, an historian with a literary bent and the art of "being there." Tim would play an active role in Ping-Pong Diplomacy (that curious match between Richard Nixon and Chou En-lai), when he visited China with the American team in '71, while gathering notes in a little plastic bag. His observations always seem to pounce on some essential detail, some oddity, whatever it was. I couldn't have crafted this book without Tim . . . and Tim's writings, which are often chaotic and contradictory, because they're uncensored and capture a particular moment, a particular place, without trying to correct himself, or whitewash his own demons. For this I'm deeply grateful.

Marty Reisman was the first of my ping-pong heroes. Dick Miles was the second. They're the greatest players America has ever produced. Both of them should have been world champions. But some trick of fate or character flaw denied it to them. No matter. They're still uncrowned champs, larger *and* smaller than their accomplishments, the basic cruelty of any sport. I'm indebted to them and that New York pride and stubbornness, which is close to criminality: they're creatures of the night who loved to gamble on their own games. Most of the gambling is gone, just as ping-pong has literally disappeared from New York and moved into the mountains of Colorado, the playlands of Las Vegas, and the convention centers and sculpted swamps of south Florida.

Ping-pong had once been an unruly sport that the U.S. Table Tennis Association couldn't quite control: it was constantly feuding with Reisman and Miles, suspending them, admonishing them, even when they won. Graham Steenhoven, a former executive at Chrysler, who ruled over ping-pong as president of the USTTA, never got along with these two "bad boys" and would probably have banished them forever if they hadn't been so damn good. It was a familiar tale. America vs. Manhattan. And America won. . . .

But this book is a tale of two cities. It was in Paris where I would enter my dotage "battling" kids of fifteen, where I would grow obsessed with the rubber on my racquet, develop lasting friendships with other players, until the very idea of a team would become part of a personal fabric, I who'd never been on a team before, who was like a wild animal, a lone wolf with a social calendar that revolved around the hours and the whims of those guardians who had a key to our club: they were much more important than publishers, editors, or college presidents, who didn't have the power to determine where and when I could play. . . .

ONE

The Farmer's Daughter

"Whenever I find myself growing grim about the mouth; whenever it is a damp, drizzly November in my soul," writes Herman Melville in *Moby Dick*, "I account it high time to get to sea as soon as I can." But I'm not a sailor and I can't even swim. When I feel my own damp November, I grab my sports bag and rush to the Bastille, where my ping-pong club is located, on a little side street. I represent the subway workers of Paris and their gathering of clubs, Union Sportive du Metro. I play in a little league, against aggressive youngsters who have a serve that's so wicked, I can barely see the ball. But it doesn't matter. My own special racquet is like a samurai's blade, masked with soft rubber pimples that's called a picot. I can neutralize *some* of the youngsters, who can't seem to solve the riddle of my bat. Others tear right through the soft rubber mask. But it's a curious sport, where graybeards like myself can compete against the young killer sharks and sometimes win. I live for the sound of the ball, the pock my racquet makes while I bend my skinny knees. The fierce concentration pulls me into the fabric of a whirlwind. I dance. I dream . . . .

It all started when I was ten. I was in a country orchard, on a farm where I picked blueberries to earn my keep. My parents must have deserted me for a little while. The farmer's daughter was basking on the orchard table, in a tank suit with the top rolled down. I did everything I could not to stare at her breasts. I didn't succeed.

Her name was Muriel, and she must have been nineteen. Country girls married very quick in those antique years right after the war (it was 1947), and

Muriel was considered an old maid. She fed me and washed my clothes while I picked blueberries under a murderous sun. And I was having a bit of a respite.

"Game time," Muriel told me. I arrived with a box of equipment from the farmer's storeroom, which was filled with cobwebs. Muriel must have noticed that I was ogling her, but she pretended not to care. She climbed off the table, opened the box, and that's how my history began. There were two sandpaper racquets inside, a lumpy celluloid ball, and a net that was as porous as the cobwebs in the farmer's storeroom. Muriel plucked on her shoulder straps and suddenly the tank suit had a top.

"Muriel, what's this junk?"

"Ping-pong, you dope."

I helped her fasten the net. It reached across the farmer's weather-bitten table, which was large enough and long enough to house six or seven sunbathers. It was like batting a ball across a hockey field. But those first "pocks" off the scratchy sandpaper unsettled me with their merciless music, as if a metronome had been built inside my ear. Muriel was up to something. She wasn't watching the ball. I was her "beard," put in place to fool the farmer. Muriel had another sort of recreation on her mind.

I heard someone whistle. A soldier appeared from behind an apple tree. All his insignias had been ripped off. He had stubble on his chin, and I guessed what he was: a deserter who'd sneaked out of the grass to make love to Muriel. I wasn't quite sure what that meant, *making love*. But it had something to do with Muriel's lowered tank top and her sunbath on a table.

"Kid, say hi to Jeff . . . and don't bother us. You play ping-pong."

"But I don't have a partner."

"Partner yourself."

Muriel seized the soldier's hand. He didn't budge. He looked at me with all the pity of a man who'd been around destruction.

"If my father comes," Muriel said, "you tell him I went to pee in the tall grass."

She took Jeff into a grotto that was completely hidden from the outside world. And Melville's dark November gripped me in the middle of July. I was bluer than I'd ever been. Abandoned with a little celluloid ball. I was Muriel's sentry, on guard near the grotto. And then, like an apparition, the soldier reappeared.

He picked up the bat, stood across from me, on the far side of the table. "Let's hit a couple."

He taught me how to hold the bat with my thumb high on the handle. He'd served in Alaska, had been the ping-pong champion of Rat Island, in the Aleutians. I volleyed with him. He put a spin on the ball that left me lunging like a feeble child. But he wasn't showing off. He was revealing the mechanics of ping-pong. He corrected my strokes, and we began to have a little dialogue with bat and ball.

Jeff belonged to a community of outlaws that I wasn't old enough to comprehend. He didn't carry a knife or a gun. He didn't wear a mask. He was a hustler, a hobo, a sharp who traveled from place to place like some pied piper enchanting folks while he fleeced them. He was also a night owl. Jeff appeared in our orchard under that brutal sun to capture the farmer's daughter. He could have been mean to me. What interest did he have in Muriel's slave? Perhaps he recognized a fellow outlaw. And it was a gift he was passing on to me, the art of ping-pong.

Muriel seethed at the attention I got. "Jeff, he's nothing, a blueberry boy."

"Blueberry boys can breathe."

And he continued with the ping-pong lesson. "Never look down when you're on the table. You stare into your opponent's eye. Games are won and lost before a single point is scored. Ever read Dick Tracy? Fearless Fosdick is your ideal player."

"But I never saw Fearless with a ping-pong bat."

"Means nothing. He has a player's mentality."

The farmer showed up, carrying a pitchfork. Jeff went on volleying until the pitchfork was inches from his throat. Then he ripped the net from the table, twirled it around the fork, utterly confusing the farmer, while he kissed Muriel on the mouth, winked at me, and strolled out of the orchard.

The farmer had a fit. He slapped Muriel, broke the sandpaper racquets, and ordered me back to the blueberries. But my banishment didn't last. Mom remembered that she still had a son and brought me out of slavery.

My skin remained dyed for a month from all that berry juice. It was worth it. I had a vocation. Ping-pong. But there was no equivalent of U.S. Metro in my corner of the world, no club where nine and ten year olds could train twice a week, do calisthenics, and learn to smash a ball. How different my life could have been. I wouldn't have had to lock myself inside a jungle growth of words. I'd have had fifty years of continuous ping-pong, not the broken banisters and rails of a writer's craft.

I had to steal a game whenever I could. In the cellar of some settlement house, or in my junior high school gym. I had no one to correct my strokes. I hadn't progressed very far from my first and only lesson with Jeff the pirate. I was a wild, erratic player without much of a backhand; it's as if my brain only had enough cunning to accommodate a forehand drive. I was crippled, incomplete. But I fell into the dream of the game, that magical mixture of silence and sound.

I entered tournaments sponsored by churches and synagogues. There was always a child prodigy who was ahead of my game, and I could never win anything but the consolation prize, for lasting the longest against whatever little wizard was around.

I enrolled at Columbia College in '55, joined the naval reserve officers' training corps. I had to spend most of my afternoons at NROTC headquarters, tolerating curses, advice, and fingers in my chest from the Marine corporal who was meant to groom us and make us into perfect cadets. Headquarters had one compensation; it was near the ping-pong room in Hartley Hall.

I wouldn't touch any of the hard-rubber racquets that lay about the room. I brought my own racquet—two sheets of balding sandpaper on a wormy stick—that was older than any cadet (it was already ancient when I swiped it from a YMCA in the East Bronx). The ping-pong–playing cadets weren't prepared for my finesse with sandpaper. Still, they had an advantage over me. You can drive a ball with tremendous speed off a bat with a rubber face. You can cut under the ball with savage precision. The pimples in the surface of the rubber will collapse against the ball and allow you a maddening underspin that ought to paralyze a cadet with sandpaper in his fist. But these boys hadn't played in Bronx tournaments. They didn't understand the psychological benefits that cling to sandpaper.

Without the cushioning of rubber pimples, the ball comes off sandpaper with a dead pock that is guaranteed to upset a player who hasn't familiarized himself with this kind of noise. I would stroke the ball with an unvarying rhythm that put creases in the foreheads of my fellow midshipmen; they would throw their rubber racquets at the wall in frustration and glower at me.

These successes didn't last. My naval science instructor caught me cheating on a quiz. I was court-martialed, evicted from the NROTC.

I HAD A RELAPSE OF thirteen years, living without ping-pong. I creaked through eight semesters of college, got married, and ran out to California to work with freshmen at Stanford University on a government project that suffered from a fit of creative insanity: it longed to discover *Middlemarch* and *Moby Dick* in the language of eighteen year olds. I failed the project. My boys and girls wrote sentences with thick, mealy strings on them. You couldn't have pulled Melville out of their sentences, or mine.

I came back to New York City without a wife. It was July 1968. Isolated, morose, I stumbled onto the Riverside Table Tennis Club at Broadway and Ninety-sixth. The club was under the street, in the windowless basement of a movie house. You walked down a flight of stairs thick with beetle shells and candy wrappers, passed through a green door with scars in the wood, and entered a long, dingy room that was ventilated by a wheezing air conditioner. You had to suck for air, or give up ping-pong at the Riverside Club. The basement had a slanted floor, and the club's seven tables existed in a lopsided world. Ping-pong bats and hunks of cardboard were stuffed under their legs to prevent customers from growing seasick at the tables. There was a corridor on the left side of the club, a gallery with camp chairs, protected by a rail, for kibitzers, ping-pong aficionados, drifters, housewives, and hobos coming out of the rain. The club was partial to strangers. You couldn't fall down and die under one of the lopsided tables without being noticed. Ping-pong aficionados had a curious camaraderie: no one ever felt stranded inside the club's green door. Much of this hospitality came from its owner, Marty Reisman, once the best ping-pong player in the world. Reisman was in an exile I couldn't understand. Lean as a jackknife, with long fingers, a wicked slope to his shoulders, and a beebop cap sitting on his skull, he didn't have the sickly aura of retirement about him. Even in his body shirt and fashionably tight pants, he could smack a ping-pong ball past your eyes (without upsetting the cap) before you had the chance to lift your paddle. He chose to play the clown. He would volley with a pretty girl, hitting the ball from behind his back, or knock cigarettes off the table with a perfectly timed shot. And he was friendly to waifs like me.

Reisman had a hard rubber bat. Seeing him chop at the ball, I was embarrassed to use sandpaper from the Bronx. So I taught myself to play with rubber pimples. I chopped, I smashed with my elbow held high, I developed terrific sidespin, and began to haunt the club. From two in the afternoon, when Reisman's opened, until midnight, I was under Broadway, listening to the bounce of ping-pong balls. I had an infallible method for determining the hours of the day: the splinters in the cellar door grew dark around dinner time.

I played Hungarians who were prominent in the ping-pong circles of Eastern Europe up to World War II, and I beat them all, old men in undershirts, with medallions on their chests. I destroyed housewives from West End Avenue, crazy enthusiasts who brought their children and their dogs into Reisman's basement and abandoned them for endless games of ping-pong. But I got unlucky in my third week at the club. I lost to a ten-year-old boy. His bat was much thicker than mine, and multilayered, like a fat sandwich that could suck in the ball and fling it back at me. My slams meant nothing; my sidespin was feeble against the soft flesh of the sandwich bat.

I growled at the boy. "What the hell is that?"

"Sponge," he said.

"Where can you buy it?"

"Paragon's." Then he looked at me. "Ask for a Butterfly."

I ran down to Paragon Sporting Goods on Eighteeenth Street and got my Butterfly bat, paying sixteen dollars to the clerk. I was mortified. Sixteen dollars for two pieces of sponge on a wooden board, and a handle painted black.

It took weeks to educate my hand and eye to the properties of sponge. I couldn't control the Butterfly; the ball sank in, then spun off the table. The Butterfly had its own pull. It was a weapon with idiosyncratic ways; either you adjusted to them or you returned to pimple rubber.

I fell in with a gang of "serious" players: a mathematics professor who grunted at you from his end of the table; a millionaire shirt manufacturer who arrived at Ninety-sixth Street in a chauffeured car and shucked off his two-hundred-dollar jackets in Reisman's beetle-infested changing room; a junkie who had an iron grip at Reisman's tables and shivered soon as he walked away from the club; a psychoanalyst who sketched flowers between games; and a black postman who had to wear a truss whenever he played.

There was a rapacious democracy about this gang; the psychoanalyst had no sway over the postman, the junkie, or the shirt king. The pecking order came from your performance at the table. I remained near the bottom, mystified by the postman's serves, unable to get around the junkie's topspin, and a victim of the mathematics professor's power attack. I could trounce the psychoanalyst, none of the others. We arranged tournaments among ourselves. We allowed nothing to intrude upon our lives at Reisman's. Ping-pong was our devotional. The junkie might have broken into half the newspaper shacks on upper Broadway scrounging for dollars, but he wouldn't have borrowed a dime from any of us. We didn't care if the psychoanalyst ate salads with Paul Newman, or had tea with Bette Midler. We never bandied stories about occupations, habits, and interests away from Ninety-sixth Street. We talked ping-pong. Was Sriver sponge superior to the Mark V? Did the Butterfly handle rattle too much? Where could we get the best price on a gross of Nittaku balls?

We had a craziness for ping-pong that reached beyond our families, our enemies, and our friends. The rhythm of a ball flying between two sponge bats kept us alive. We would have shrugged our shoulders at regular tennis. It was much too slow for us. Our eyes couldn't have tolerated the Brobdingnagian dimensions of a tennis court. We needed a nine-by-five table, a tight green net, and a pale ball that could squash under our heels, at Marty Reisman's.

It was sponge that helped bring about Reisman's doom. Reisman wouldn't gab. I had to go to the shirt king, who collected all sorts of apocrypha on ping-pong players. He'd become the club historian and the folklorist of Reisman's exile from international competition. The shirt king confused names, countries, players, and dates, but his stories had a consistency that couldn't have been found in an almanac, or ping-pong book.

"Marty got swindled," he said. "Nobody could touch him in those days. Not Miles, not Leach, not Bergmann, nobody. Miles had the backhand, I admit. He could defense you into the ground. What strokes. Did you ever see Miles bend his knees? He could exhaust a mule. But not Reisman. Marty had a trigger in his thumb. He hit bullets. You could lose your eyebrows playing with him. And what happens? The Japs invented sponge to take revenge on Reisman. They snuck in through the window at the internationals, in '53. It was Manila, I think, or maybe Singapore. They call Marty 'the Needle' because he's that thin. He wipes out the whole field, Serbians, Romanians, and Swedes. Then he has to play the Jap. This Satoh holds out his sandwich bat. What could Marty do? Miracles don't happen in Singapore. You can't mix pimples and sponge, that's the rule of the universe. We lost, and the Japs walked home with everything."

"Okay, that's one tournament," I said. "Why didn't Marty switch to sponge?"

The shirt king ruffled his nose with great scorn. "Sonny, when you're the greatest in the world at twenty-five, and they steal a title away from you, you don't go and join them. They tell you your bat's no good. Pimples are dead. Why should you believe them, just because they happen to be right. Sonny, what d'you say?"

I had no profundities for the shirt king. I was a sandpaper champ who had adopted the pimple bat at Reisman's club and was weaned away from it after three weeks. Now I was a hypermodernist, dependent on the Butterfly. I couldn't have returned a mediocre serve without my sandwich bat.

I WAS UNDONE BY outside accomplices. My name had been stuck inside a fat book prepared by the government teaching project at Stanford University, and prep schools, churches, and colleges began inviting me to speak on the artistry of freshman composition. I was appalled. Herman Melville had been asleep for eight years (I uncovered no geniuses at Stanford University). But those invitations were a powerful medicine to me. They arrived on formidable stationery, with the logos of individual schools, and the offer of seventy-five dollars a day.

I said goodbye to Reisman and took my sandwich bat on the road with me; no one wants to get caught flat-handed in the ping-pong parlors of South

Carolina and Tennessee. I was in great demand at certain military academies of the South and Southwest. I had plenty of tricks. I raised up Herman Melville's corpse at these gatherings, as I promised my cadets that each of them had the power to write with their own dark, maddening vision. "There is a single voice in all of us," I said, my face cleft with shadows falling from the curtains behind the dais, to give me the proper show of gloom. I grabbed my seventy-five dollars and ran.

Ping-pong was my only solace. I played wherever a table could be found: in pool halls, private homes, insane asylums, and church recreation rooms. None of my opponents had ever seen a sandwich bat. They tripped over my perfect strokes. I could have taken on a busload of players after any of my talks. I needed the sound of ping-pong balls to drive the humbug out of my head. At least I had the wisdom not to play for cash. You can get your knuckles smashed sharking in a strange town.

I returned to New York in a month's time. Melville and military schools were lousy credit at Reisman's place. My successes on the road meant nothing to the gang of "serious" players. I was a mongrel in their eyes, a worthless character who allowed external affairs to cheapen his obsession for ping-pong. They hit among themselves, barring me from their tournaments. "Seventy-five dollars a day," I piped to the shirt king. "Couldn't be helped . . . lectures . . . for the government."

The shirt king was disgusted with this mention of money. He wiped his bat with a paper towel. "Sonny, did you hear me cry about the disappearance of button-down collars? A ping-pong freak can lose his credit rating soon as anybody. You're not my accountant, so why should I complain? Do us a favor. Walk away from here."

I had no choice. I sat in the gallery with the Butterfly between my legs. Reisman noticed my miserable state. He offered to hit with me. Whatever the rules about mixing rubber and sponge, I couldn't do much against Reisman's slams and chops. He ate me alive with his pimple bat. I wouldn't have swiped three points from him in a tournament game. Staring across the table, I began to comprehend his exile. He'd grown up with rubber pimples, going through tournament play, then some international federation legitimized the sandwich bat, and Reisman was left without his weapon. Was he frightened of having to "relearn" the game? Maybe so. But it had to be more than that.

Rubber pimples make a puny weapon. Reisman's eye and the whip of his arm were more important than any bat. But sponge had altered the game. The player with the stronger bat was most likely to win. My Butterfly could demolish sandpaper, pimple rubber, and low-grade sponge. If it failed me, I would look for a bat with a faster, trickier face. Technology thrived in the "new" ping-pong: the weapon determined the man.

This was fine for middling players like me. But why should Reisman pay homage to the sneaky gods of the sandwich bat, who could bite at you according to the different qualities of sponge? He sat out the tournaments, retired to Ninety-sixth Street, shot cigarettes off a table.

And I realized why I was drawn to Reisman. I'd met him before . . . in a country orchard circa 1947. Reisman was almost a reincarnation of Jeff, that pirate who'd given me my first lesson. Both of them were mavericks. Reisman had been thrown out of several championship matches after he got caught betting on himself. He was writing a book, *The Money Player*, his confessions as a ping-pong hustler and racketeer. But my affinity was much deeper than the romance and charm of an outlaw. Hardship, and defeat had humanized Reisman, made him part of a small band of men (and women) who watched over each other. And Reisman had welcomed me into his band. It didn't include Muriel, the farmer's daughter. She might still be in some orchard, sunbathing without her tank top. But one thing is certain: my life as a ping-pong player began with a touch of eroticism, a striptease that wasn't meant for me. . . .

TWO

The Needle

GAMES OFTEN HAVE mysterious ancestors and myths. Ping-pong is no exception. The game seemed to arrive with the twentieth century, but its real antecedent is *jeu de paume*, or royal tennis, the oldest of all racquet sports, though the first "racquet" was a monk's palm. *Jeu de paume* (or handball) dates back to the eleventh century, when it was played inside the monasteries of France. Monks used their bare hands to slap a ball of hair, cork, or wool, covered in sloth, over a makeshift net. But these monks were ingenious. They found that a leather glove was much more efficient than a bare hand and lent the ball a greater velocity and spin. Soon they attached cords and tendons of gutted animals to the fingers of their gloves, which allowed them to have a higher, sweeping shot. They then attached these cords and tendons to a frame, added a handle, and *jeu de paume* was now a genuine racquet sport, which spread from the monasteries to the courts of princes and kings. The church tried to ban tennis but it was too late. There were almost two thousand tennis courts in France by the thirteenth century.

Henry VIII, who ruled England from 1509 to 1547, was addicted to the game. He couldn't survive without his own tennis court. He had one built at Hampton Court Palace around 1530, with lavish balconies, grilles, and "penthouses," so his entire retinue could watch him play. Supposedly he learnt of the execution of Queen Anne Boleyn, one of his unwanted wives, while he was in the middle of a match. He was a frightful gambler and nearly brought his house to ruin by betting on himself. And legend has it that another king, James I, hoping to flee from assassins, couldn't hide in a particular drain because it was clogged with old tennis balls.

Royal tennis was also popular during the reign of Louis XIII, France's melancholy king. In Richard Lester's film, *The Three Musketeers* (1974), we can find Aramis and Porthos playing *jeu de paume* against two other musketeers at one of the king's tennis courts. The racquets seem remarkably modern. The players wear white caps to protect them from the sun coming through the windows. There are no real boundaries. Aramis and Porthos wallop the ball against the ceiling and sidewalls and win the match. . . .

Jeu de paume was played by aristocrats on the king's men-of-war. And the tennis court built at Versailles in 1681 nearly bankrupted the nation. By the middle of the eighteenth century *jeu de paume* had already begun to fall out of favor and disappeared from France during the revolution. It would reappear in the nineteenth century, both in England and France, but was quickly shunted aside by a new racquet game, lawn tennis, which arrived around 1873, and didn't require elaborate buildings and the sponsorship of kings and queens. The sport was an instant success. The first championship match was held at Wimbledon in 1877. And game manufacturers tried to cash in on the popularity with some form of miniature or "pocket" tennis that could be played in the parlor. One such game, with its cork balls and battledores (the long-stemmed racquets used in badminton) was called Gossima, to suggest the light, floating cobwebs of an English garden. Other variations used rubber balls. And British Army officers had their own "table tennis" with carved champagne corks, cigar box lids as racquets, and books lined up to serve as a net. But none of these parlor games lasted very long. The racquets were clumsy and too big; cork balls weren't lively enough, and rubber balls were much too wild to be used indoors; only knitted balls could avoid "broken windows or a bloody nose," but knitted balls had no bounce.

Table tennis languished until a prominent English athlete, James Gibb, brought back a box of celluloid balls from America. These balls had a perfect bounce and were "featherlight." It was Gibb who first noticed the game's signature sound, the "ping" of the celluloid ball against a vellum battledore and the "pong" of the ball as it bounced on the table. And ping-pong was almost born.

In 1901 English sports manufacturer John Jacques registered the name "Ping-Pong," and sold the American rights to Parker Brothers, another sports manufacturer. But there was still the problem of an outsized racquet. Soon the long-stemmed handle shrank, and wood replaced the parchment and string of traditional battledores. At first the wooden blade was covered with leather, felt, or cork, but *none* of these covers seemed to liven or complicate the path of a celluloid ball.

In 1902 an English player, E. C. Goode, during the intermission of a London tournament, happened to notice a pimpled rubber coin mat at a local drug store. Goode had a bit of lightning in his brain. He purchased the mat and covered his racquet with it, producing a distinctive spin to the ball. Goode won the tournament with his new hard-rubber bat. "Serious players quickly realized the additional spin and control offered by the textured rubber surface," according to table tennis historian Charles Hoey.

Still, ping-pong was hardly a sport. It was considered an after dinner amusement, played by rich and poor. Between 1901 and 1903 "the game caught on like wildfire." A factory in Essex produced two-and-a-half million balls a week. There was an epidemic of ping-pong poetry:

The craze spread to the nursery soon,
The children there, each afternoon,
Discarding corals, bibs and rattles
Gave bottles up for Ping-Pong battles!

There were pictures and postcards of men and women playing ping-pong in the most fashionable places, wearing fashionable clothes. A well-dressed ping-pong "couple" were featured on the cover of *The Ladies' Home Journal* (October 1902). But by 1904 the game "was put on a shelf" and virtually disappeared. It was revived in the 1920s, during the jazz age. Parker Brothers held tournaments in the Waldorf-Astoria, with extravagant cash prizes. Celebrities such as American tennis champion Bill Tilden and German boxer Max Schmeling would arrive in tuxedos to watch the games. But a rift developed between the Parker Brothers Ping-Pong Association and some of the more serious players and aficionados, who formed the International Table Tennis Federation (ITTF) in Berlin in 1926, with Ivor Montagu as its first president. The federation couldn't compete with the prizes that Parker Brothers could offer. But its tournaments had much less of a circus quality, and more and more players began to bolt . . . until Parker Brothers' prizes had no meaning at all.

In '33 the United States Table Tennis Association (USTTA) was founded, and ping-pong would become a *visible* sport, particularly in Manhattan, which had its own emporium and ping-pong parlor, Lawrence's Broadway Courts, located above an automobile showroom at 1721 Broadway, between Fifty-fifth and Fifty-sixth Street. Lawrence's had seven tables on the second floor and five other tables on the third. It had once been a speakeasy owned by Legs Diamond, "the most shot-at man in America." Reporters followed Legs Diamond wherever he went. "He danced, he laughed, he wore the best, and moved with the fastest," writes William Kennedy in his novel about Legs Diamond (*Legs*). Women were crazy about him and his "wide-brimmed white felt hat." He was the most elegant and vicious bootlegger in town. And Legs' Manhattan hangout was at 1721 Broadway. There were bullet holes in the walls, a souvenir from the times when Jack Diamond's speakeasy was raided by other bootleggers or the cops (who often served as bootleggers themselves). But these bullet holes were more than a rude reminder of Legs Diamond's nights and days. He left a much larger legacy: a bit of the freewheeling, chaotic life along the Stem, as Diamond's stretch of Broadway (from Times Square to Fifty-ninth Street) was known. Anything could happen, and often did. Diamond was already dead when Herwald Lawrence, a black man from Barbados, opened his ping-pong parlor. There were no more bootleggers or bullet holes, but Broadway was still a very private country, where single men and women—dancers, actors, gamblers, musicians, prostitutes, and ping-pong players—crept out of their boardinghouses and hotels all along the Stem. Ping-pong players were very much a part of the culture. They practically lived at Lawrence's, which was open half the night.

The very best players in America—Dick Miles, Sol Schiff, Lou Pagliaro, and later Marty Reisman himself—would enter Lawrence's Friday night tournaments, which soon became legendary enough to be written about in *The New Yorker*, and columnist Murray Kempton would capture this culture in an article for *Esquire*: "The reality is that ping-pong players are the ultimate amateurs of American sport: their only secure cash source comes from taking bets against each other." And betting was what

Lawrence's Friday night tournaments was all about . . . and the sheer deviltry of the sport. "Life is no longer work as ordinary people know it; one's work is the casting of spells, the making of demon music, one's travels vagrant, one's living the product of cunning; in short, one has become a gypsy."

And Lawrence's gypsies ruled their corner of Broadway. As Dick Miles, ten-times U.S. champion, said of Lou Pagliaro: "Unlike us, he got married, got a job, bought a house and raised a family in Brooklyn. . . . There was always something strange about Lou."

But the American players didn't have Parker Brothers behind them. And the USTTA could barely raise the cash to send them to world championships. There were *no* American players at Cairo (in 1939), the site of the last world championship until after the war. But America's insulation from world-class tournament play had one positive effect. "We didn't know how good we were," said Reisman. "We just played and played." Refugees from Hitler's war soon ended up at Lawrence's, and Lawrence's Friday nights began to take on an international flavor.

"Table tennis started out, about fifty years ago, as a slow, piddling game for old ladies," Marty Reisman told *The New Yorker* in 1960. "The Hungarians were the first to bring elegance and style to it. Then the Czechs came along with the concept of the rocklike defense. A point would go on and on until someone made a mistake. In one match, a single point lasted over two hours. After the Czechs, Dick Miles . . . and I speeded up the game terrifically. We introduced the quick hit—slamming the ball before it reaches the peak of its bounce."

Since world tournament play was utterly disrupted during the war, Lawrence's became the symbolic home of ping-pong, a kind of Rick's Café, where exiles could mingle with the rash young Americans. Some of the best players, like "Dixie" Cartland, would be drafted, but Miles had a heart murmur and Reisman, born in 1930, was much too young to fight in a war. And so he fought in Lawrence's, particularly against Miles, the only one who could regularly beat him. That's when he was nicknamed the Needle.

The war years were *almost* a kind of idyll. Players couldn't gallop around the country to different tournaments, because of wartime travel restrictions. They had to meet at Lawrence's, gamble on important games, test themselves against whoever was available. For Reisman, who was living with his father in a downtown hotel, Lawrence's *and* the Stem had become his real address. He remembers the Automat on Forty-seventh, where he could feast on blueberry pie for ten cents, Lindy's, where he would gobble cheesecake like a king; the Capitol Theater on Fifty-first, with its bandstand and little storm of chorus girls. "The streets were packed with soldiers and sailors in uniform." Reisman and other Lawrence regulars would play exhibitions for wounded war veterans. A chauffeured Army limousine would pick him up at his father's hotel and drive him from base to base.

But the Needle felt forlorn when he wasn't picked to go to Paris in 1947, for the first world championship since the war. The American men's team consisted of Miles, Schiff, and Pagliaro, three of Lawrence's Friday night greats. They didn't win any medals in Paris, but they played superbly against the Hungarians and the Czechs. Suddenly the Americans had arrived. And they soon ranked second in the world, right behind the Hungarians. "It came as a pleasant surprise to us all in New York that our Friday night tournaments, which were considered almost family affairs, was competitive with the best table tennis played overseas."

Reisman did make the team that went to London for the world championship of '48. He was seventeen, a bumpkin who'd never been abroad. "What a thrill it was to stand in the lobby of the Royal Hotel and see the great table tennis players of the world, men whom I had read about and dreamed about and admired, if only vicariously, for years."

Reisman's idols included defending world champion Bohumil Vana from Czechoslovakia, who had "an electric quality about him on the table as he moved rapidly from position to position . . . Vana covered almost the entire table with his forehand. He was able to do so because he stood far to his left side of the table, and because he was tremendously quick." He was also very, very poor. He had to sell his own trophies to keep alive.

There was Alex Ehrlich, a Polish Jew, "tall and big-boned," thirty-five years old. He'd spent four years at Auschwitz, where Nazi officers happened to recognize him as a ping-pong champion and kept him out of the gas chamber. He was assigned to the job of defusing bombs in the vicinity of Auschwitz. "Once," according to Reisman, "Ehrlich was defusing a bomb when he found a honeycomb nearby. He smeared the honey all over his body and when he got back to camp, inmates licked the honey off his body for nourishment." Whether Ehrlich had ever been a human honeycomb or not, he was a formidable player.

But the most formidable player at the championship was Richard Bergmann, an Austrian who had taught physical education to the Royal Air Force during the war and was now a British subject. Stocky, muscular, "he had legs like fire hydrants," but he could dance around the table "like a doe." He'd been banned from the Paris championship for trying to professionalize the sport. "His idea was to form a professional table tennis league," which would have been an immediate threat to the ITTF. But he was back in business at the London games, "perhaps the fiercest competitor" ping-pong has ever known. The Needle had to face him in the fourth round of a tournament packed with ten thousand people.

Bergmann danced around the Needle, outfoxed the seventeen-year-old wild child from Manhattan, and won the fifth and deciding game of the match by suddenly taking to the attack before Reisman could get his own "kill shot" into motion. Bergmann went on to win the finals against Bohumil Vana, and the Needle sailed home aboard the *America*.

He trained for an entire year and returned to Europe in January 1949, with Dick Miles and "Dixie" Cartland, for the world championship in Stockholm. The Needle was determined to win. He got as far as the semifinals, when he had to play Vana. The Needle was already preparing his victory speech, but Vana "beat me in three straight games . . . and broke my heart."

Reisman was scheduled to play in the British Open the following week. This time he went all the way to the finals, where he would meet Victor Barna of Hungary, "who had been World Champion before I was born." Barna was the Babe Ruth of ping-pong, a five-time world champion who'd performed in exhibition matches at the London Palladium and the Rainbow Room in Manhattan. But he was thirty-six years old, and "slightly over the hill."

The Needle had a new strategy. "I decided to pretend that I was back at Lawrence's playing Miles . . . for money." He clowned a bit against Barna, who "had a metal plate in the wrist of his racket hand, the result of an automobile accident." The Needle beat Barna in five games, the first and only American ever to win the British Open.

London critics had a love affair with Reisman and his "forehand kill," which they called "the Atomic Blast." But the USTTA was much less enamored of Reisman and his shenanigans. "The Danny Kaye of table tennis" was fined two hundred

dollars for moving into a classier hotel and forcing the English Table Tennis Association to foot the bill and was suspended indefinitely from competition, "not only in the United States, but all over the world." He'd broken ping-pong's "courtesy code."

The Needle had to wait three years before he could play in another world championship. But it was almost by accident. The USTTA didn't have enough money to send a team to Bombay. But Reisman and Dixie Cartland, who happened to be touring Germany at the time, crept onto a charter flight that was leaving Frankfurt for India with most of the European players. It was 1952, a fateful year for ping-pong and Marty Reisman, who was considered a heavy favorite to win the men's championship. Bergmann was getting old and fat. The Needle was sharper than he'd ever been. At twenty-one, he hadn't lost his Atomic Blast.

Neither Bergmann nor Reisman won. Hiroji Satoh, with his horn-rimmed glasses and his pigeon toes, was considered the poorest player on Japan's team. But he was the only one in the world to use a racquet with a thick layer of rubber foam, which muffled the sound of the ball. "Bergmann had spent a lifetime studying the sounds of table tennis. But against Satoh there was no sound . . . Bergmann was a deaf mute in a game that required dialogue."

Reisman fared no better against Satoh's sponge bat. "I was throwing lethal punches and hitting myself in the face." However hard Reisman hit, the ball flew back at him with twice the speed. It didn't help when he tried to slow down the game. The ball still went on eerie flights. "Sometimes it floated like a knuckleball, a dead ball with no spin whatsoever. On other occasions the spin was overpowering."

Satoh was the new crown prince of ping-pong. A million people welcomed him when he returned to Tokyo. The man with pigeon toes was almost as popular as the emperor. No other Japanese had won a world championship of any kind since the beginning of the war.

There was a great deal of sound and fury about banning sponge rubber from future tournaments. But nothing happened. Suddenly the manufacture of table tennis equipment became a multimillion dollar business. One man, Bernard Hock, had manufactured by hand most of the hard-rubber racquets used by Reisman and other champions. But a Hock bat could last a lifetime. Sponge had to be replaced after forty hours of play. Manufacturers grew very fat. Within a year, more and more players switched to sponge. But the other masters?

"The sponge paddle destroyed Richard Bergmann," Reisman told the *New York Times* in 1960. Bergmann "was unable to adjust his timing and tactics to the new weapon. He became, like many silent picture stars after the introduction of sound, a has-been overnight."

Or, as Murray Kempton laments: "Ping-pong seems to be one of those intricate little civilizations that is subject to periodic catastrophes at the hand of mad inventors."

But Hiroji was no mad inventor. His "soft" bat seems one more evolution in a game that evolved from other games and constantly keeps reinventing itself. Sponge rubber transformed ping-pong "from a graceful game of careful calculation into a high-velocity battleground," as Lisa Lipkin observed in the *Daily Forward*, evoking the time when ping-pong "was the sport of choice among thousands of Jewish boys growing up in New York in the 1930s and 1940s, a time when Jewish men dominated the field."

But it was an old-world game with an old-world charm, practiced in Budapest, Prague, and the most European city of all, 1940s Manhattan. And the charm disappeared forever in Bombay. As Kempton mythologized the Needle: "To come upon Reisman is like finding some perfect specimen of a lost classic age, thin as a blade, the step a matador's, the stroke a kitten's."

And America seems mired in that age. For a while the USTTA tried to outlaw the sponge racquet; that only distanced American players from the rest of the planet. There were no more Marty Reismans and Dick Miles in the new era. The current French champion, Jean-Philippe Gatien, or "Philou," has his own Atomic Blast, slamming the ball off a very low bounce, but Philou doesn't have Reisman's raffish grace. He's a professional, almost the way Richard Bergmann imagined the sport would become: a "theater" in which players could earn their living, and not have to sell their own trophies.

Ping-pong is played by over two-hundred-fifty million people all over the world, with forty million tournament players, a fraction of them from the United States. There are more ping-pong clubs in France than there are players in the USTTA. Ping-pong has been totally marginalized in America. The best players have to train in pool halls, with two or three ping-pong tables. Lawrence's is like a lost dream of an older, wilder Broadway. And when Riesman's club closed in 1980, the victim of Manhattan's real-estate boom, I had to sheathe my Butterfly and forget about ping-pong.

Unlike football, ping-pong "fails to evoke blood." We have "little use for the delicacies of a sport in which a 138-pound man can reign supreme."

I suspect that American ping-pong suffered a deep trauma in Bombay. Had Reisman won the world championship— in spite of Satoh's bat— his charisma, his ability to please a crowd, might have popularized ping-pong in America, because the Needle would have found a way to hypnotize with his Hock bat. Americans love a fairy tale, but not one that ends in failure. . . .

THREE

The Girl Who Looked Like Ginger Rogers

LAST JUNE THE NEEDLE INVADED Britain with a couple of other Yanks and challenged a team of British veterans to the first hardbat competition between the two countries since 1952, and the arrival of sponge. The match was played on Denmark Road in Manchester. The Brits won, but novelist Howard Jacobson, a *pongiste* himself, felt that watching the Needle and listening to the sound of his hard-nippled bat was like "beholding Caruso before the invention of the gramophone."

Jacobson remembers the stories he'd heard about a prior invasion, when the Needle and Dick Miles had come to England over fifty years ago, "and brought to European table tennis . . . the slick glamour of New York, and exhilaration, a conviction that as long as you were on it, the table tennis table was the centre of the universe."

And Jacobson mourns the loss of that glamour. Like Reisman and so many others, he's convinced that sponge has "ruined both the spectacle and the aesthetic" of a game that "has become too fast, too furious, too technical, too private . . . With lumps of mattress in your hand"—i.e., the sandwich bat—"you do not play the old virtuoso game of cat and mouse, you do not fence for an opening, and you do not stand in another room retrieving smashes," as Richard Bergmann delighted in doing.

Players like Reisman, Miles, and Bergmann had once "packed arenas to the rafters. Table tennis touched a nerve in post-war Europe, with its "jumping indoor intensity. . . . It appealed to swotty boys like me because it felt intellectual. An activity for philosophers," like Bergmann, who collected trophies and lived from hand to mouth. . . .

One of the Brits who demolished Reisman & Co. on Denmark Road was Jacobson's boyhood idol, Jeff Ingber, "the most dashing man I'd ever seen."

Jeff is a diabetic who plays ping-pong. Without his two insulin shots a day he would no longer be alive. When his sugar level gets low in the middle of a game, he will stop to eat a bar of chocolate and then continue the match. He lives in Manchester, where he was born sixty-five years ago, and grew up on the mean streets of Cheetham Hill. He's a textile merchant who started playing when he was ten, at a local Hebrew school, which had one table inside a shed. But that table must have had a miraculous tilt. By the time he was fifteen Jeff was the number-three ranked "junior" in all of England. It was 1951, just before Satoh's Big Bang in Bombay. He watched Bergmann battle Vana at the British Open, held in a Manchester amusement park. Bergmann went through "boxes and boxes of balls" before he would select the one he liked. He was a complicated character, "full of bits and pieces." He put "clocks under the table," so that he could track himself in relation to the twenty-minute rule: whoever was ahead after twenty minutes would be declared the winner of a game. Bergmann was "a wonderful fighter," who destroyed his opponents "with fitness and footwork" . . . and the help of his clocks.

But the younger players didn't copy Bergmann or Vana. They'd watched the Needle in 1949, "and immediately modeled themselves on the American style of hitting," on Reisman's "snap forehand drive" and "devastating attack." Jeff himself switched to squash and didn't return to ping-pong

. . . until Marty came to Manchester in 1988 for a match. The best of the modern players never appealed to Jeff. "The top Europeans and the top Chinese are all robots with no particular identity." But not the Needle. Playing in his checkered pants and Panama hat, he performed his own rapid-fire ballet that "can charge the atmosphere of an entire hall . . . it was Marty who inspired me to take up the game again. There isn't anybody like him."

Jeff picked up his old "Barna bat," with its Dunlop rubber and Victor Barna's signature on the handle. "I got it out of mothballs to make my comeback . . . I never changed my bat in thirty-five years."

But the spirit of ping-pong has changed, of course. There are fewer and fewer young devotees: the majority of Manchester's best players are all over thirty-five, like Howard Jacobson. I had to remind Jeff that he's still a lucky man. Ping-pong has disappeared from Manhattan. There isn't a single club around. If I want to test my picot against Reisman's hard rubber bat, we have to scavenge like hawks to find a table. The Needle is half blind at the moment. He has cataracts in both eyes. But he still insists on playing. We end up at a luxurious East Side health club, where the Needle is treated with a certain noblesse. He contributed his own table to the club. It's wheeled out of a storage room and we start to play. It's enough that Marty can hear the pock of the ball against my picot, and follow its flight with his narrowed field of vision. The ball arrives out of a blur and he delivers his old Atomic Blast that rockets right through my racquet.

Sound is *everything* to the pimple player. During the thirties and forties, the age of classic ping-pong, there was actually a blind referee who could call every shot by the sound it made off a particular bat. His name was Chuck Medick. "He could be at a tournament where fifteen tables were in use simultaneously, and he would remark: 'What a fantastic game that is on table nine,'" Reisman writes in *The Money Player*. "Medick had the most sensitive ears in the world, and he was as enthusiastic as any fan. He was like a sensitive radio antenna, tilting his head from side to side to hear if the ball hit on the table. He got carried away at times and applauded a particularly good volley. . . ."

My own volleying stinks. I can't crack Marty's defense. Half-blind as he is, Marty says in the thick of play, "I can see the label on the ball. What appears to be blinding speed to the audience is like slow motion to me." And why shouldn't I believe him?

He still talks of the movie that's *about* to be made from his book. The real problem is: who could play Marty but Marty himself? The book's subtitle is a bit misleading: *The Confessions of America's Greatest Table Tennis Champion and Hustler*. Dick Miles might not appreciate Marty crowning himself the table tennis king. But whatever the quality of Miles' game, he never had Marty's charisma. Miles, as Jeff Ingber notes, was "a deadpan player," who couldn't ignite a crowd the way Marty could. And according to another ping-pong maven: "Miles lacks color and is not interesting to watch . . . his forehand drive is a clock-like motion, so well groomed it's monotonous."

The Money Player reads like a Dickensian fairy tale. Marty has been revising that fairy tale in interview after interview. "Reisman has carved a dozen lives for himself with a pimpled rubber racquet and a rum runner's wits," Dave Hershey wrote in the New York *Sunday News Magazine* in 1971. "He has won and lost fortunes from here to Rangoon." That's the mask that the Needle loves to wear. The table tennis toreador and king of the cool. Playing for money is "just a way of getting the adrenaline going. What I like is the sense of surviving under fire, of living as a matador. I see the ball as the tip of a bull's horn—superb table tennis is like what bull-fighters call 'close work,' when you dance within goring range of the ball. Money simply enhances the danger factor."

But there's a deep wound under all that dancing.

The Needle was born on February 1, 1930. His mother, Sarah, was a Russian refugee. His father, Morris, drove a cab. Marty grew up on East Broadway, in the heart of the Jewish ghetto, Manhattan's Lower East Side. "It was feast or famine in our house, mostly famine." Morris, who was also a bookmaker and a compulsive gambler, had once owned a fleet of seventeen cabs. "I saw him lose six taxies during one session of poker." Morris would later lose them all.

"I had a nervous breakdown before I was nine. I was so insecure I felt I was going to die, was obsessed with the thought that my heart might stop at any minute. It reached its culmination one day at school. I felt my eyelids flutter. . . ."

Marty fainted and woke up in Bellevue. "It was a horror house," with kids who screamed or fell into total silence. Marty fooled his doctors, hid his anxieties as well as he could, and was out of Bellevue within a month.

But these anxieties would take another form, crippling headaches that might blind Marty in the middle of a match. He couldn't cure the dilemma of his own parents. They would battle all the time. They separated when Marty was ten. First he lived with Sarah and then with Morris, at the Broadway Central on West Fourth Street, where his dad played poker. It had once been the prince of Manhattan hotels, where railroad tycoon James Fisk was shot to death by another tycoon, in an argument over the favors of a gorgeous actress, Josie Mansfield.

Meanwhile Marty, who suffered from astigmatism, was told by an opthamologist to play ping-pong in order to strengthen his eyes. He picked up a racquet at the Educational Alliance, a settlement house on East Broadway, which was heavily endowed by comedian Eddie Cantor, another "alumnus" of the Lower East Side. The Needle was eleven. He had a natural gift for the game. "I never took a lesson in my life." By the time he was thirteen he was city junior champion and was already "a money player" who'd discovered the art of hustling, as he grabbed nickels, dimes, and dollars from whoever was dumb enough to bet against him at local parks and playgrounds. At fourteen he drifted up to Lawrence's, which was soon his training ground, his gambling casino, and his permanent address. From the moment he arrived, Marty began to bet. In a couple of years he was eating steaks at Lindy's and earning two-hundred-fifty dollars by betting on himself at Lawrence's Friday night tournaments. And when he got to London in 1948 as part of the American team, he hustled nylon stockings and ballpoint pens, which were impossible to find in postwar Europe.

After the USTTA suspended him in 1949, he and Doug Cartland barnstormed with the Harlem Globetrotters, the mythical black basketball team, owned and managed by Abe Saperstein. Professional basketball was almost an invisible sport in a country dominated by baseball and football. But the Globetrotters weren't invisible at all. While white basketball struggled to survive, the Globetrotters began to tour the world as basketball artists and clowns. Marty and Doug would perform at halftime, keep five balls in action during a single game. Marty was almost as big a clown as "Goose" Tatum, who could hide a basketball under his shirt while he was dribbling up and down the court. The Needle would abandon his racquet and hit the ball with his eyeglasses, a Coke bottle, or a shoe and play Doug with pots and pans.

After three years, they left the Globetrotters and toured on their own. "You can't name a maharajah I haven't played for," Marty would boast in his book. He had a habit of catching history by the tail. He and Cartland happened to be in Hanoi on May 7, 1954, during the debacle at Dien Bien Phu, when the French were defeated by the forces of Ho Chi Minh . . . and played a match in Thailand right in the middle of an earthquake. "I thought it was applause," Marty said of the rumblings around him.

"My whole life has been flirting with danger." He was "Errol Flynn with pimpled rubber, carving up the world," according to Dave Hershey. And when Reisman took over the Riverside club in 1958, he continued his career as a money player, taking on anyone who would challenge him. "It's like going out there in a hail of bullets."

Marty began entering tournaments again. He discarded his hard rubber bat at the U.S. Nationals in 1960, played with sponge, and won the singles championship. But it didn't bring him much pleasure. "Before the introduction of sponge there was a dialogue between the two players that most people could understand. A top attacker, probing like a chess grandmaster playing white, might move ten or twenty or thirty times, all to set up checkmate, the kill shot."

It's ironic that Bobby Fischer, one of the greatest chess champions of all time, also played ping-pong, *and* at Marty's club. "Fischer played table tennis the way he played chess: fiercely, ferociously, going for his opponent's jugular. He was not a bad player, though his style was awkward and unorthodox. He had awesome concentration." Reisman remembers him as "a killer, a remorseless conscienceless ice-blooded castrator. . . ."

And Reisman himself? Did he ever play "white" as fiercely as Bobby Fischer? Perhaps all his exploits in *The Money Player* were a kind of bravura that kept him from playing "white." There's almost a mock exuberance to Reisman's many scams, and the late historian and literary critic Peter Shaw picked this up in his review of *The Money Player* for the *Westsider*. "Contrary to popular belief," Shaw wrote, "autobiographies tend not to reveal but to conceal the truth—from their authors no less than from their readers." Supposedly successful men (and women) "turn out often secretly to have regarded as failure much of what their autobiographies proclaim as success."

For Shaw, Reisman is not really "the hustler he thinks himself. He lacks the killer instinct that he rightly sees as the key to success in a man like Bobby Fischer. Lacking the necessary touch of inhumanity, Marty Reisman has been something less and something more than a world champion," a man whose "true story lies in defeat."

And so much of his charisma comes from this edge of defeat. He often wears a wide-brimmed white felt hat when he plays, just like Legs Diamond, another man with a killer instinct. But Reisman is a much kinder and sadder gypsy than Diamond ever was. And therein lies his charm . . . and his power, that fragile, crazy elusiveness of a lost world champion.

THE UNITED STATES DID HAVE a world champion in ping-pong, only it was a woman rather than a man. Ruth Aarons, born with show business in her blood. Her mom, Leila Hughes Aarons, was a light opera singer, and her dad, Alfred A. Aarons, was a New York theatrical producer who'd helped put on George Gershwin musicals such as *Lady Be Good* (1924), *Funny Face* (1927), and *Girl Crazy* (1930). Ruth discovered table tennis by chance, almost stumbling upon the game. It was 1933, in the middle of the Great Depression. She was fourteen, a blue-eyed blonde with the look and poise of Ginger Rogers. She was playing tennis on the roof of a Manhattan hotel when it started to rain. Ruth drifted down to the basement, discovered a ping-pong table, and out of boredom batted the ball around. She was hooked right away. And within months she was playing in tournaments, a little blonde bombshell who startled spectators by appearing in "sky blue pantaloons equipped with hip pockets for extra balls," while most of the other women players wore dresses that practically covered their ankles.

She would win her first U.S. Championship at fifteen, and Ruth would always practice with men, so that she could quicken her own game. "I came cheap," one of her male partners would say. After hitting the ball with Ruth in the family's Riverside Drive apartment, he might get a "sandwich served by the butler and two tickets to a Broadway show."

The USTTA couldn't afford to send her to Prague in 1936 for the World Championships. Ruth paid her own ticket and was chaperoned by her grandmother. She crossed over on the *Manhattan* with other members of the American team, practiced on the promenade deck, and "passed the hours by watching motion pictures, eating gumdrops, dancing during the evenings, or playing Monopoly."

Ruth wasn't a self-conscious diva about the costumes she would wear at a match. She was already enrolled at the Taphagen Art School, where she studied dress design. "She's an artist," her dad said. "And she designs gorgeous gowns." After the Americans arrived in London for a warm-up match with the Brits, Ruth got carried away with her "fashion-passion," according to Tim Boggan. She *had* to collect "bellboy buttons" for one of her costumes. So she began chasing bellboys across the lobby of her London hotel. . . .

Ruth marveled at the *seriousness* of table tennis among the Brits. In America it was a ragtag sport, a parlor game for amateurs. But in London there seemed to be "a thousand clubs."

Both the public and the press adored Ruth's dazzling defense and were "surprized, amused, and intrigued" by her "well-cut bags." And when the women's team walked around Prague in their playing slacks, "a silent, gaping crowd" followed after them, as if they were creatures from the moon.

The 1936 World Championship was held at Lucerna Palace, a four-thousand-seat "bunker" with three balconies. The Czechs were passionate about their own team and would swarm "onto the playing floor, interrupting matches at will." But Ruth was prepared to play Maria Kettnerova, a twenty-three-year-old Czech, who was the defending World Champion. Kettnerova would defeat Ruth during the Corbillon Cup team matches. "The roar that went over the Lucerna as the final point was scored might well have been heard in Chicago."

Ruth would confront her again in the semifinals of the women's singles competition. "I lost the first game and nearly went to pieces." She was also having difficulty with the Czech fans. Their sideline seats were a little too close to the table, and Ruth had to dance around like a demon or she couldn't have returned Kettnerova's "deep drives." Ruth steadied herself and won the second game. She was ahead 20-18 in the third, when Kettnerova "hit a kill so hard it seemed impossible to return and wheeled in relief from the table," only "to have Ruth from deep court do the impossible and get it back with her opponent completely out of position. Even the Czechs went wild at the shot."

Ruth went on to win the match and face Germany's Astrid Krebsbach in the finals. Krebsbach's "dreaded backhand" couldn't unravel Ruth, and suddenly there was a new world champion: seventeen-year-old Ruth Aarons of Riverside Drive.

All of Prague was crazy about Ruth. Even America was a *little* excited when the U.S. team returned to New York. One reporter noted that Ruth had "the color, poise and grace of a finished fencer."

She found herself famous, the ping-pong champion who looked like Ginger Rogers. With her father's show business connections, Ruth put together a table tennis floor show. Her partner was Sandor Glanz, an Hungarian immigrant who was a former champion. It was Sandor who had prepared her for Prague. "Until I met him, I used to kill the first shot in a rally, but he has changed my technique so that now I build up slowly for one big kill."

On July 27, Ruth and Sandor opened at the Rainbow Room and were an enormous success, even though an hour before their act the table hadn't arrived. Ruth called a local sporting goods outlet, "and as all their trucks were out, a taxi was sent dashing up Fifth Avenue through red lights," with a green table "reclining on top."

The show consisted of one 21-point match and the offer of a quart of vintage champagne to anyone who could win against Ruth with or without a handicap. On one particular night Ginger Rogers herself caught Ruth's act.

In 1937 Ruth would appear at the British Open in "R.A.F. blue trousers with chromium buttons and a crushed strawberry shirt." In the finals, against Kettnerova, she was down 2-0, but rallied to win "the hardest match I ever played in my life."

One former world champion, Lazlo Bellak, would claim that the driving force behind Ruth's success was that women players simply weren't "strong enough to maintain an offensive game against Ruth for a full match." She could whirl and dance like no other lady.

But Ruth got into trouble after the match. She remained in London to prepare a fifteen-minute act with "Michael French," alias Michel Glikman, a former French champion. They would appear in the dark at the May Fair Hotel cabaret, their bodies revealed in silhouette by means of hidden lights. The ball and the net seemed to be "illuminated, while the players" could "be picked out by their white berets, white gloves, and white shoes."

But both the English Table Tennis Association and Ivor Montagu, president of the ITTF, disapproved of the exhibition, declaring that Ruth, who'd come to England to play in an international match, could not accept "any engagement for professional entertainment" without ITTF approval, which she had never bothered to get.

England's own *Table Tennis Activity* defended Ruth, noting that "she was news. Pictures and stories about her appeared daily in almost every national newspaper." Ruth had "gained more publicity for the English National Championships than any other individual player . . . The sooner it was possible for a steady income to be made by those skilled in the arts of the game the better."

Montagu suspended Ruth. But it didn't really matter very much. Ruth would retire at eighteen to become an entertainer. She'd already been on the cover of the February 22, 1937 issue of *Life* magazine and "she was not going to sully her past achievements, her box office name with the inevitable losses that would come under the pressure of competition," according to Tim Boggan.

In 1938 she would appear at the Boston Arena with Lou Pagliaro and other ping-pong greats. Four thousand people showed up in the middle of a storm . . . to watch Ruth Aarons. She was "so much the focus of everyone's attention that reporters seemed to think she was the only player on the court."

"I'm going to Hollywood," announced the girl who looked like Ginger Rogers. "I have studied singing and can dance a little, may be able to break into the movies." But she never did.

She performed at Boston's Ritz Carlton Roof, where Red Sox slugger Jimmy Foxx, a ping-pong enthusiast, challenged her to a game. She destroyed him like a kindhearted killer. "Jimmy has excellent timing and a good eye," Ruth said, "but he has no idea of this modern table tennis and the importance of spin."

In 1942 *Colliers* would write about Ruth: "In a game which featured lanky, wizened males, and chunky, horse-faced females, she stands out like Betty Grable in a Home for Aged Spinsters."

In 1945 she toured the Persian Gulf, India, and Palestine for the USO. After the war she would become a booking agent for Shirley Jones, Janis Paige, Celeste Holm, and other actresses. She died in 1980. . . .

She's forgotten, of course, except among ping-pong mavens. She grew up in an era of aviatrixes, of women golfers, such as Babe Didrikson, and movie goddesses, and seemed to capture the public's imagination while she played in a crushed strawberry shirt, and for a little while ping-pong itself, embodied in Ruth Aarons, began to have its own importance, its own beauty and grace. But ultimately it was one more novelty act, at least in the United States.

Ping-pong could never bring in the big bucks, and that's why it was always doomed. It thrived best when mavericks like Marty Reisman had their own ping-pong clubs, which served as a home for all the gypsies in the neighborhood. But when Marty was "locked out" of Manhattan, when his club closed in 1980, this was also the end of an era. Ping-pong had nowhere to go, not even underground, in one last cellar on Ninety-sixth Street.

FOUR

Gentlemen

"THE PING-PONG PARLOR IS just an externalization of your soul," one aficionado, who happened to be a nuclear physicist, told Marty Reisman. "Constant movement, constant turmoil. It's a womb to you."

But the womb disappeared, and all of us suffered. "I didn't mind losing my fluorescent tan," Marty lamented. "What hurt was that our whole subculture had disintegrated."

We walked around with a funeral face, burying our Butterflies and our Mark Vs. There was no other sport that could engage me in the least, not swimming, not golf . . . nothing but a bit of paddleball that I played at my local handball court in Greenwich Village. There might have been a paddleball culture, but I wasn't part of it. And the big, bulky racquet with its taped handle had neither charm nor elegance. It was like holding a caveman's club. I had to survive without the pock of a celluloid ball . . . .

I was moving to Paris, bit by bit. It was 1992, not the good old days of cheap rent and *atmosphere*, when La Coupole was a dump that sold wood and coal to keep you from freezing your ass off in the winter, and the Closerie des Lilas was a simple café where young Hemingway worked on the terrace with a blue notebook and an unsharpened pencil, reshaping American fiction into short sentences that were like lonely little islands. And now the Closerie has a barstool with Hemingway's name on it, and no Hemingway.

I was scribbling at home when I got a call from musician Georges Moustaki. He'd heard from a mutual friend that I was a ping-pong freak, and

Georges invited me to play with him at his club, U.S. Metro, which was then located on the rue Pascal, near the Mouffetard, a winding, hilly market street Hemingway had adored.

I'd brought an old Butterfly with me to Paris, and this is the racquet I used. Georges kept a key to the rue Pascal, and we had the club to ourselves. We would play in the morning, then eat at a little restaurant on the rue Candolle, Les Delices d'Aphrodite, owned by the Mavrommatis brothers, a tribe of Greek Cypriots.

The entire summer passed like that. I'd rediscovered ping-pong, ping-pong in Paris. At first Georges could toy with me. He had a much more wicked racquet than mine, and he'd been playing twice a week at U.S. Metro. I went to a table tennis equipment store and replaced my old peeling sponge with Mark V skins. I marveled at the way the young Chinese merchant peeled off the old skins, scraped ancient glue from both sides of the wooden blade, applied fresh glue from a little pot, and rendered me some kind of killer king with my Mark V. I returned to the club, played Moustaki, and now we would have marathon matches that could last from morning to late afternoon, with Mavrommatis in the middle.

Georges was a mongrel like me, a wanderer, a *métèque* who was born in Alexandria. His father, who was Greek, owned the best French language bookshop in the Middle East, La Cité du Livre, where actor Louis Jouvet would visit, along with Jean Cocteau and young Lawrence Durrell. Georges would sit on the balcony and read Sartre, Kafka, Gide, along with current crime novels, when he wasn't playing ping-pong at his local sports club. He arrived in France at seventeen, without a penny in his pocket, did odd jobs, sold books door-to-door, became a bartender, a pianist at a piano bar, and started to write songs. And in '69 he appeared on a television show, *Discorama*, sang "Le Métèque," and was suddenly famous all over France.

> *Avec ma gueule de métèque*
> *De juif errant de pâtre grec*
> *De voleur et de vagabond . . .* *

> (* With my mug of a métèque
> Of a wandering Jew and Greek shepherd
> Of a thief and vagabond ...)

It was hardly a protest song, but it seemed to capture the spirit of May '68, when an entire generation of students began to feel like vagabonds and métèques, adrift in French society. And Moustaki had become the voice of this vagabondage. We would often sit at Les Delices d'Aphrodite, almost thirty years after the May uprisings, while a band of women at the next table would serenade Georges with words from "Le Métèque."

But after '69 Georges went on his own vagabondage . . . to Los Angeles. He worshipped Henry Miller and visited the old master in his modest house at Pacific Palisades. Miller was almost eighty, and Georges, who could barely speak English, felt like a mute. "Do you want to play ping-pong?" Miller asked with a modest grin.

Moustaki was convinced he could beat an eighty-year-old man. But Miller was "a fiendish player." He annihilated Georges and then lost all interest in him. Moustaki had to quit Pacific Palisades with his tail tucked between his legs and no words of philosophy from the master.

In 1981 he was invited to participate in the Tournoi des Gentlemen, sponsored by various federations, clubs, and sporting goods manufacturers to raise money for cancer research and bring attention to *le ping*. It was a tournament of stars, where actors, journalists, composers, athletes, and rock singers could battle it out on ping-pong tables at Coubertin Stadium in the sixteenth arrondissement. Georges lost very quickly, "was wiped out." He felt humiliated. A young journalist at the stadium, Elisabeth, noticed Georges' plight. She gave him his first racquet, taught the métèque how to play. . . .

He'd entered three more Gentlemen's after that and was in training for a fourth when I first encountered Georges. Gradually I was introduced to other players at the club, a retired jockey, a baker, an ex-convict, a wine merchant, a repairer of dolls, a hawker at a flea market. But U.S. Metro wasn't a world unto itself, like Reisman's; it was more like a summer and winter camp, where players prepared themselves for tournaments. Most of them were "ranked," that is, part of a mandarin system that was often hard to follow. I was *outside* the system, the lowest of the low, a drudge who wasn't even classified. I had the letters NC stamped on my license: *non-classé*. Georges was *classé*, and had the right to exist. He would go on to win the Gentlemen's, beating Eddy Barclay, record producer and ex-jazz musician, who'd arrived at the tournament with his own trainer. And Georges was our local hero, the first player from U.S. Metro ever to grab the title.

Suddenly there was a great deal of furor over table tennis in France. Jean-Philippe Gatien, "Philou," would become the world singles champion at Gottenburg, Sweden, in 1993. Philou was twenty-five years old, a left-hander who hit the ball very low off the table, like Marty Riesman. But Philou's Atomic Blast had come with sponge. His topspin was "crueler" and much more savage than any other player's. He was born in Ales, a little town near Nimes, was a ping-pong prodigy at eleven, and went to live and train at INSEP, the National Institute of Sports and Physical Education, in the bois de Vincennes, at the edge of Paris. It's a veritable school for champions. There was no such school in the United States, no national center of sports, particularly not for ping-pong. There'd been Lawrence's for a while . . . and Marty Reisman's, without sports doctors and trainers, colleges and lycées where the young wizards could attend. I was left-handed, like Philou, but I'd learned to play in a country orchard, and there were no country or city leagues where I could have developed, no scouts or coaches who could have whisked me away to the bois de Vincennes.

But I did have one little piece of luck. Jean-Louis Fleury, who was among the highest ranked players at our club, happened to be a comic book fan, and he'd read *The Magician's Wife*, a graphic novel I'd done with artist Francois Boucq . . . about a young girl who's mesmerized by a magician, marries the guy, abandons him because of his cruelty, and then helps to save his life. Jean-Louis was a diabetic, like Jeff Ingber, and had to eat candy bars during a competition or collapse at the table. He grew up in the center of France and progressed so quickly at his local club that soon he had no one to train with. But he hadn't come to Paris as an eleven-year-old, like Philou, and prepared himself for championship play. Instead, he studied art at Aix-en-Provence, moved to Paris, exhibited his paintings at local galleries, and taught art at various junior high schools in the meanest suburbs of Paris. He was on U.S. Metro's number-one team. I loved to attend his matches. I'd become disenchanted with professional sports, like baseball and basketball, where millionaires grappled in some make-believe world, and wouldn't move a finger without consulting their business managers. I longed for the days of Sweetwater Clifton, who'd left

the Harlem Globetrotters in 1950 to join the New York Knickerbockers, a roughhouse team that didn't play for big dollars.

And Jean-Louis' matches reminded me of the ancient Knicks, even though basketball and ping-pong had little in common. But there was a free-wheeling fury, a level of deep concentration, and delight that bound both teams in my mind. I'd become the mascot of U.S. Metro One. If they were short a man in a match they couldn't win, I'd play on the team as a kind of kamikaze. I was like some kid who was suddenly allowed into the presence of grown-ups. And under Jean-Louis' eyes, I played like a demon, defending and attacking against local champions who couldn't initially "read" my unorthodox style. I stood like a flat-footed chicken and chopped at the ball with my Mark V. Of course, after six or seven points, these champions solved the riddle of my game and demolished the mascot of Metro One.

It was Jean-Louis who noticed my obvious flaws: I was a *defenseur* with an attacker's weapon in my hand. He advised me to switch to a picot, with its devilish pimples that would throw off my opponents, neutralize their spin, and hurl back the most powerful smash with unpredictable speed. That didn't stop the local champions from continuing to kill me. But lesser players had a much more difficult time. And I felt like the little samurai of the rue Pascal, a street named after the philosopher whose *Pensées* I'd devoured as a boy, because he understood the limits and the loneliness of humankind.

I had to return to the States to work on the film adaptation of my novel *Paradise Man*, about a hired gun named Sidney Holden, who was much more chivalrous than anyone around him. I wrote in the office of my Russian producer, right above Carnegie Hall. It was the fall of 1994, when Moscow was a boomtown, part of a new Wild, Wild West. And the producer, who'd come from Moscow, was himself involved in all the mysteries of export-import. He couldn't return to Moscow without five or six bodyguards. I saw him as one more métèque, like Moustaki and myself, mongrel America's new Jay Gatsby. He had a house on Long Island, like Jay, but he wasn't quite as metaphysical as Scott Fitzgerald's man. He played the guitar, wore eyeglasses, and didn't have the same pinch of romance. Still, I wanted to weave him into our film, turn him into some prince of the Russian Tea Room. But I didn't have the time.

I was scheduled to play in the next Gentlemen's Tournament. Elisabeth, Moustaki's former coach, had registered me. She must have thought that a novelist had some sway among movie actors and rock stars. I had dreams of winning the Gentlemen's with my picot. I couldn't train in New York, without Jean-Louis. I returned to Paris, a bit worried that my Russian producer might hire his own hit man and have me followed to Coubertin.

I arrived at the players' gate, was immediately given a tournament T-shirt, a pair of sneakers, and a bat. I undressed in a locker room among French actors whose names I couldn't recall. I discarded the tournament's bat, which was meant for beginners and babies, unsheathed my picot, walked through a kind of bullpen with the other combatants, and entered an arena lined with rows of green tables. I could have been at some gladiators' fight to the finish. The people in the stands were cheering their own particular champions. I noticed Moustaki. He had a wistful look on his face, as if he were trying to tell me something I should have figured out for myself. The Gentlemen's was pure show business, a spectacle in the guise of a tournament, and I was a gladiator who hadn't even graduated from gladiators' school.

I played a gentle giant in the first round who was hoping to have a little fun at Coubertin. I wiped him off the table with my own instinct to kill. He slouched back into the bullpen. I crucified my next opponent with tiny flicks of my picot. I was prepared to climb over a pile of corpses to the ultimate round of the tournament. I begged the gods of ping-pong that I wouldn't have to play Georges. Winning or losing would have been close to incest, like crushing our family tree. But I never got near Georges.

The Gentlemen's announcer, who looked like a slick car salesman, approached me before my fifth match. He was examining a slip of paper, signaling to himself that my appearance at the tournament had been some kind of big mistake. There was no category for novelists at Coubertin.

I won the match. But I knew something was wrong when I saw Elisabeth whispering to several of the tournament's officials. Perhaps she and Georges were the only ones at the stadium who had ever bothered to read my books. She'd begun to cry.

My next opponent appeared at the table. It didn't take me more than a second to realize my fate. He was a spoiler, the tournament's hit man, put there to keep the unfamous out of the finals. He also happened to be the player-coach of Metro One. Call him Hervé.

We warmed up a bit. I had this insane idea in my head that I might be able to beat him with willpower and some witch's magic wand. He trifled with me, let me score nineteen points, so that the gallery would have a bit of excitement.

I sat down in a terrible funk. Hervé played in the semifinals against a former soccer hero, Luis Fernandez. In spite of my gloom, I was amazed at Hervé's own magic, his ability to keep the game close. It was match point, and what if Fernandez stumbled, hit the ball into the net? But Hervé had absolute control. He could have been holding Luis Fernandez by the hand.

Fernandez played Moustaki in the finale. He defeated Georges in a very close and elegant match.

And the crowd had the finals that it craved: a pair of superstars who understood how to entertain.

The ushers dismantled the tables, rolled the last one into the center of the arena, and Philou played an exhibition match with Patrick Chila, his teammate at Levallois, and the second-best player in France. The crowd adored Philou . . . and Patrick Chila. They thumped at the ball, returned impossible shots, spun around like merciless ballet masters, and I realized that Reisman had been wrong: ping-pong had to evolve into a faster, attacking game, with cowboys who were very, very quick on the draw.

Then two old-timers appeared, former French champions who might have gone back to Reisman's era. Both of them had big bellies. They must have had the Needle and Doug Cartland in mind, because they played with pots and pans, kept five or six balls afloat with miraculous drives. It could have been halftime with the Globetrotters. History moved in maddening circles that not even Einstein could predict.

Ping-pong was different, and ping-pong was the same.

FIVE

A Man Called Methuselah

"THIS IS MY SEVENTIETH YEAR of ping pong playing," Henry Miller writes in *My Life and Times* (1971), a couple of years after Georges Moustaki's visit to Pacific Palisades. "I started at the age of ten on the dining room table. The focal point in my house is the ping pong room. I take on players from all over the world. I play a steady, defensive Zen-like game. The importance of this recreation lies in preventing intellectual discussions. No matter how important or glamorous my opponent may be I never let him or her distract me."

And Miller played all over the world, at his father's tailor shop on Fifth Avenue, at Clichy with Anais Nin, with Chaim Soutine at the Villa Seurat, with Lawrence Durell in Corfu, at a Paris bistro with Brassaï, in Hollywood with Man Ray. . . . He's probably the most celebrated *pongiste* who ever lived, not so much because he happened to write *The Tropic of Cancer* and *Black Spring*, books that astonish us with Miller's endless appetite, but because he has made of ping-pong an emblematic, life-and-death game, a *struggle* that both relaxes and exhilarates, and was absolutely essential to him.

If he became a kind of guru at Big Sur and Pacific Palisades, a little Zen master pirouetting on the ping-pong table, that's because fame itself had turned him into a freak (like Hemingway in Havana). In *My Life and Times*, we find a photograph of Miller in his ping-pong room, racquet in hand. He seems to be using sandpaper, but it's hard to tell. Certainly he would have used sandpaper in the Brooklyn of Decator Street in 1901 and 1902. He's wearing a pink shirt and a leather vest at Pacific Palisades, like a drugstore cowboy. His opponent is a barefoot blonde. She's naked, and we catch her from the rear. She can't distract the old master, who seems to be looking into some deep abyss.

In his own way, Miller has *immortalized* ping-pong, transformed it into a spiritual exercise, which can enlighten eighty-year-old men (and women) and reward their concentration with a peaceful vigor. Miller played until the day he died. And if he was, as George Orwell described him, "a mere Jonah," who lived outside politics, in the belly of the whale, I still can't imagine him without his ping-pong table. One thing he taught us was that ping-pong was good for the soul.

We've entered the new millennium, and nothing much has changed . . . except that U.S. Metro has moved from Philosophy Street (the rue Pascal) to a little alley off the boulevard Richard-Lenoir. Moustaki no longer has a key to our club. I'm forced to play at U.S. Metro in the middle of the afternoon. I dream of Henry Miller in *his* Paris, borrowing salt and pepper at the Villa Seurat from Soutine, who was already "suffering from stomach and liver trouble and whatnot, and lived like a recluse." I'm also a recluse. It's only ping-pong that can get me out of my eagle's nest above Montparnasse (my apartment sits right over the cemetery).

I'm a little jealous of Georges. It has nothing to do with his songs. I wish I had been able to play with Henry Miller. I went on a little pilgrimage to the Villa Seurat, found number 18, where he'd lived in the same house with Soutine. It's an Art Deco building that looks like a boat. But there isn't a plaque on the wall, *nothing* to suggest that Henry Miller or

Soutine had ever been there. That's the fickleness of history. But I can still conjure up Miller's ping-pong table in some imaginary garden behind number 18, can hear the pock of his steady, diabolic strokes. Would I have been able to bamboozle the master, corrupt his Zen-like spirit? I'll never know. . . .

I'm a refugee from the rue Pascal, where our club was like a warehouse with a backdoor that opened onto an unbelievable garden and a stone wall with the texture of tiny jewels. Our new club on the allée Verte has no particular charm. We even have a gluing room, where the very best players can rip off the skins of their racquets, put on a coat of rapidly drying speed glue, reattach their skins with the help of a roller, and not stink up the entire club with terrible fumes. The layer of glue is an attacker's paradise, because it behaves like a catapult: the ball digs deeper into the sponge and comes back at you with a bizarre, bulletlike motion. Jean-Philippe Gatien might not have won his championship at Gottenburg without that crazy glue. It made his topspin untouchable.

But there aren't a whole lot of gluers in the afternoon, which is almost like a geriatrics' ward. There's Pierre, the baker who's in his midseventies; he's the current *senior* champion of Europe. There's René, a Japanese who was born in France and is Pierre's age; he was in Paris when the Germans arrived in 1940, and he recalls the dust on their uniforms when they appeared at the Porte d'Orleans; by the afternoon the dust had disappeared.

It's against René that I amuse myself the most, René with his penholder grip, favored by the Japanese, Chinese, and Koreans. He uses only one side of the racquet, which he grips with thumb and forefinger, and flicks out at you like a lizard's tongue. René's reaction is much quicker than mine, because he doesn't have to choose between backhand and forehand; he has a relentless forehand from

both sides of the table. We always end up having battle royals. I have to switch my game if I want to win, go on the attack, angling my shots steeper and steeper so I have a chance of neutralizing that lizard's tongue.

My trainer, Jean-Louis, has exiled himself from table tennis. He no longer has a license to compete. And my own confidence is shaken without having him around. It was Jean-Louis who could correct my constant lapses, catch each little error at the table, errors I would never see. And I realize how much raw intelligence is needed just to measure your opponent's game. But with Jean-Louis' help I have entered that mandarin system of classified players. I was no longer a common drudge. What had given me an edge was my own unorthodoxy. I played like no one else. And I felt a kind of kinship between table tennis and my scribbling, which had its own wild side, its own crazy signature, as if I were operating from a perverse part of my brain. And though I'd never be more than a middling *pongiste*, I sensed that there was the same leap into the unknown; the ping-pong paddle was a weapon, like words themselves; words could annihilate, could kill, the way Bobby Fischer could kill with some ultimate leap of his imagination, with the music of pawns and kings in his head, or the way Jean-Louis had killed while he was in competition. It was always a wonder to watch him play: the verve, the grit, that dreamlike ability to concentrate on the ball . . . and then his kill shot, his final smash, which was like the end of a roller-coaster ride where I might take a reader, letting him or her drop to the ground, with no cushion at all.

I asked Moustaki what he thought about ping-pong and music, expecting a little "bonfire" of comparisons and quotes. But Georges wouldn't play. He said that the rhythm of the ball had nothing to do with his music, though a lot of musicians were drawn to table tennis. Ping-pong was like "mathematics in space." What attracted him most was that the relationship with his partner was often "between love and hate." He would have agreed with Henry Miller that ping-pong could be active and inactive at the same time. It was meditative, "very Zen." He smiled and told me that rock stars often had a ping-pong table written into their contract to keep from getting bored on the road. Georges himself loved to play with fellow musicians before a show. "It relaxes you, gives you energy," he said. And sometimes a ping-pong table would travel with his sound equipment, or he'd find a club in Athens or Berlin where he could play. It was part of his vagabondage.

But a ping-pong club, wherever it was, also had a language of its own. When Dick Miles was growing up on the West Side of Manhattan during the late 1930s, he entered a club on Ninety-second Street and watched several world-class Hungarian players. "I remember seeing the Hungarians out there at the table hitting balls, warming up, enjoying themselves, talking and laughing in a very intimate, in-group way about their strokes and styles. It impressed me very much that they had a private table tennis language I didn't understand—that table tennis itself had such a language—and I wanted to know more."

And this became *my* language in France, table tennis talk, the one terra firma where I felt at home. I could rattle on about my *coup droit* and my *revers*, the clawlike *pince* of René's penholder grip, the wicked bounce of his *service lifté*. I could cry *merde* or *bordel* if I miffed a ball, or Moustaki would slap his own head and scream *quel âne*, the way his own teachers in Alexandria would curse and call him a dunce if he happened to mispronounce a word.

I learnt to shout *fainéant* if someone stood with flat feet and didn't hustle at the table, or cry *il m'a beaucoup gêné avec ça*, if some young wizard had a

service that was particularly bothersome. And I had to glue myself together again, or *recoller*, if I didn't want to fall behind in a game with Georges.

I'd mastered a narrow, very singular argot. I was only fluent at the table. And thus I lived in a singular world, where I could rattle an opponent, but would fall apart the instant I had to ask an operator about my telephone bill. I'd entered the culture at a curious slant, with my ping-pong paddle. . . .

I was no longer the mascot of U.S. Metro One. I was now the strongest player on Metro's eighth and weakest team. We were a bunch of Methuselahs, boys in our sixties and seventies (Roger, the oldest, was seventy-eight) battling against a field of young warriors. I'd missed a whole bunch of matches. Georges, who also played on the team, had a good excuse. He might be touring Canada, Germany, or Japan the week of a match. But I had suddenly grown anxious about traveling to some gymnase at the edge of Paris and returning after midnight. It's not that I felt the Metro was unsafe. I belonged to the Metro workers, didn't I? I was part of their Union Sportive. And traveling to those far-flung gyms had become the means of discovering a much poorer Paris, a Paris of métèques, like Henry Miller country. Often I'd play at clubs right under the Périphérique, or in the alphaville of green skyscrapers known as Beaugrenelle. But with Jean-Louis on permanent vacation from ping-pong, I'd developed agoraphobia.

I just couldn't seem to go to a match. But I gathered my courage for Metro Eight. I played in a match on the rue Milton in the ninth arrondissement, near Pigalle and the Place Clichy. I couldn't help thinking of that blind poet, John Milton, author of *Samson Agonistes*, and I wondered how "eyeless" I'd be on Milton's own block. The gym's lights had a blinding glare, and I could do nothing but blink at the ball. I lost three matches that I should have won. I was shivering at the table, like Methuselah at the end of his career. I did my own little Saint Vitus' dance. It was time to retire, to quit all competition, and sit in the corner at U.S. Metro, like Marty Reisman's blind referee, and hum to the music of every ball in flight. . . .

I complained to Jean-Louis. "Je suis maigre," I cried in my kindergarten French. "Je suis nul." He laughed at me. What the hell was one match? It was always difficult to play on another team's turf. My opponents could use the terrible lighting to their advantage. They knew all the blind spots, where and when a ball would stick in your eye. How could I abandon my team? Metro Eight had yet to win a single match. We were the laughing boys of our little league, the scarecrows, the ancient mariners who were lapped up by infants with speed glue.

Jean-Louis agreed to "babysit" for me, clutch my hand, go with me to the match. We arrived at U.S. Metro just as a gaggle of gorgeous girls had come out of the modeling agency at the other end of the allée Verte. They had a blondness and a deep blush that was much more dazzling than a ping-pong ball. Their posture was so perfect that I felt like some couch potato who was idling in their presence. How would I ever be able to concentrate again?

Jean-Louis led me into the club. I dressed for business in the changing room, wearing the club's shorts and shirt, and I hit the ball for half an hour with Jean-Louis, attacking when I could, and defending against his topspin. It was like a tonic to me, a junkie's deliverance, facing the speed and the spin of the ball. I returned shots that would normally have plunged right past my racquet. I was immortal.

But Methuselah was still shaking before his first match. I had the jitters. Jean-Louis was there to correct my strokes and point out my opponent's obvious faults. But I didn't control the tempo of the game. I won with a bit of luck and all the frustration that my picot could bring to the table.

I was steadier during the second match. But I had no rhythm. Again my picot rescued me from embarrassment. I eked out a victory like an awkward bird of prey. I wasn't nimble on my feet. I couldn't find my own autopilot, the dreamlike ecstasy that allowed me to take risks.

My last opponent had a wicked repertoire of serves and was much more accomplished than the other two. My picot meant nothing to him. He seemed to scorn my clumsy play. He was utterly bored while he was warming up. He might have been fifteen or sixteen. Little Erik.

He won the first game and then sat down and gobbled a sandwich, satisfied with himself. I was trembling and whining, "I'll never win, I'll never win." Jean-Louis had to ease my hysteria and warn me to avoid Erik's forehand, which arrived like a lightning bolt.

"Forehand?" I said. "I can't even catch one of his serves."

"You're panicking. Don't recoil. His serve is nothing special."

"Ah, I might as well sit under the table and die."

I won the second game. Erik was careless. He was munching on chocolate while he played. He mocked me by reining in his serves and his lightning bolts.

"Revanche," he said with a smile, and we started to play *la belle*, the third and deciding game.

La belle.

This time he served with a demonic crouch, hiding the blade of his racquet under his elbow, so that I couldn't see the path *or* the pull of the ball. But it didn't matter now. I flicked the ball back at him, very, very shallow, forced him to play a slow, plodding game. And when he did attack, I danced like Fred Astaire, returned whatever Erik threw at me. He wasn't prepared for the "bite" of my ball. I'd

interfered with his brilliance, tortured the torturer
. . . .

I still swear that ping-pong is like the dream of writing a book. In his *New Yorker* profile of Philip Roth, "Into the Clear," David Remnick writes about Roth's recent burst of energy, his explosion of novels from *Sabbath's Theatre* to *American Pastoral* and *The Human Stain*, as Roth was feeling his own fragmented immortality, "like the fleeting period in an athlete's life when the vectors of his physical abilities and his mastery of the game—his experience, intelligence, and imagination—meet at the highest point."

Roth had undergone quintuple-bypass surgery eleven years ago, had suffered a nervous breakdown, had separated from actress Claire Bloom, and now lived like an artist-monk in rural Connecticut. "My schedule is absolutely my own . . . If I get up at five and I can't sleep and I want to work, I'm on call. I'm like a doctor and it's the emergency room. And I'm the emergency."

While working on a novel, Roth seemed to exist outside any normal human limit, like Swede Levov, his Jewish athlete in *American Pastoral*. "I have to tell you that I don't believe in death, I don't experience time as limited. I know it is, but I don't feel it. I could live three hours or I could live thirty years, I don't know. Time doesn't prey upon my mind."

I'm not the Swede, and I'm not Philip Roth, but in that ultimate game with Erik, I'd crawled right under the arrow of time in my murderous concentration, making shots I'd never made, defying gravity to slap at the ball. And poor Erik was out of chocolate. He had nothing to assuage the grief of having lost *la belle* to old Methuselah. His little gods had failed him, gods who'd never failed him before . . . .

SIX

Hemingway's Room

I'D BEEN TRACKING HIM FOR months, though I didn't have the slightest clue about him, his credentials, or his name. I had no entrée into the upper tiers of French table tennis. I felt like Joseph K. standing outside Kafka's castle. Jean-Louis thought he might be able to help me find some subtrainer on the national team, who'd applied heated elbow pads to France's Four Musketeers—Philou, Patrick Chila, Damien Eloi, and Christophe Legout—who were among the top twenty players in the world. But not a single subtrainer materialized.

I scribbled a letter to the ITTF. A note came back with news about the head of the ITTF's sports science committee: Dr. Jean-François Kahn, who happened to work at the Pitié-Salpêtriére hospital complex, the same Salpêtrière where Charcot once ruled like a master magician, convinced that "female hysteria" could also be found in men, and where Freud had watched Charcot hypnotize his patients in 1885. I wondered if Dr. Kahn himself was some kind of alienist, who'd hypnotized the Four Musketeers and thus improved their attacking game. I had a childlike fascination *and* fear of Pitié-Salpêtriére, as if I'd be swallowed up once I entered that complex on the boulevard d'Hôpital in the thirteenth arrondissement. . . .

He was quite friendly on the phone.

I asked if we could meet in Montparnasse.

I suggested lunch at La Coupole. Dr. Kahn had never eaten there, and it astonished me. La Coupole was such a dinosaur, landmark, *and* institution, *le phare des Années Folles*, where Kiki, Montparnasse's very own artist's model, held court when she wasn't sleeping with Modigliani or Man Ray, and flirting with Foujita or Hemingway. Of course I should have realized that La Coupole was much more mythic for an American scribe than for a doctor of sports medicine at Pitié-Salpêtriére. Why should he have cared about Kiki's adventures? And how could he have known that La Coupole, until it was tarted up by some restaurant tycoon, had been an enormous, crumbling dive where Sartre ate lunch with Simone de Beauvior, and where one could order the best *pommes frites* in creation. I'd first eaten there in 1979, when I was so fascinated by a little porcelain teapot with the words THÉ ELEPHANT marked on it that the waiter offered it to me as a gift.

La Coupole also had *dancing* in its cellar, dating from 1927. It was at La Coupole's dance hall that Marlon Brando bared his cheeks in Bertolucci's *Last Tango in Paris* (1973). But I hadn't come to La Coupole with Dr. Kahn to discuss Brando's cheeks. He was a tall, youthful looking man in his fifties, with a mustache and gray hair. I wouldn't have confused him with any *alienist*. He was born in Luxeuil-les-Bains, a tiny little thermal station in the east of France that was over two thousand years old. He'd started playing *ping* at grammar school in Luxeuil, where he'd helped agitate to buy the school's first table. The girls at school were a little jealous, and young Jean-François agitated to get them a table, too. He'd played in regional tournaments while he studied at the faculty of medicine in Nancy and continued to play during his military service in the south of France, where he was in a special unit involved with civil protection. He had to prepare for "different catastrophes"—car accidents, earthquakes, and forest fires. Then he took a position in sports medicine at INSEP, the school for champions in the bois de Vincennes. He was one of the first doctors in France to specialize in table tennis. He was at INSEP when Philou arrived, a lonely little boy from Alès. "It was hard for him to be far from home." Ping-pong virtuosos often had family problems they couldn't surmount and didn't become high-level players like Philou. . . .

I couldn't help examining the terrain at La Coupole: a large Art Deco clock, chandeliers that looked like the wings of magnificent biplanes; pea green pillars with unsigned paintings from les Années Folles—lots of full-bodied women with bare breasts, or black masks, and a coiffure in the shape of a devil's horns. Nakedness seemed to abound at La Coupole. The brasserie's own emblem was a nude model with a helmet of black hair, books, a bottle of wine, her toe stuck in a painter's palette, like Kiki of Montparnasse. . . .

Dr. Kahn began to lead a peripatetic life when he became official doctor of the French national team for fifteen years, from 1977 to 1991. He sat on the bench with the team, lived at the same hotel, and now, as chairman of the international sports science committee, he continued to travel. He'd just come back from the world team championships in Malaysia, where the Musketeers had done so poorly against Taipei, a team they should have gobbled up. "They lost the first match in their mind," he said. "They weren't ready to fight and win."

The Musketeers had been plagued with injuries. World-class ping-pong was a grueling sport. It was "violent to the body," particularly for "attacking players," like Gatien and Patrick Chila, with "many rotations, many spinning movements of the trunk." Chila had back problems, and Philou had a serious problem with his hip. The Musketeers had "overcrowded calendars, playing nearly every week, often several times a week."

Philou was in his thirties now, and with his special style of hitting very close to the table, he had an additional strain on his trunk . . . and a topspin that had lost a bit of its savage slide. "After thirty the time you need to react to a ball increases and your speed decreases." A slightly older champion had to "analyze very well to compensate for decreasing physical ability . . . if he wanted to remain in world-class competition."

But it wasn't simply a problem of France's battered Musketeers. Dr. Kahn discovered "back and knee pain in young girls." Women players had a particular problem "with their ankles and knees." He discovered "shoulder, wrist, and back problems among women and men, depending on age." There was a question of "compartment syndrome . . . As the muscles get larger because of exercise, they can produce pain." And it was Dr. Kahn's job "to find the origin of this pain." There was also the problem of "isometric contraction in the legs." When you maintained a certain position without moving in the middle of a game, the blood pressure began to build. "Blood pressure will increase in short periods of time because of isometric contraction."

I began to feel more and more like Methuselah worrying about the isometric contractions I might have to endure during my next match. But we turned to another subject: speed glue. He told me that during a tournament, Gatien would change the rubber on his racquet after each match, which meant that he and the other Musketeers were constantly regluing their racquets. Dr. Kahn and the rest of the ITTF were in favor of outlawing the glue. "The first reason," he said, "was the reason of health." Some of the players "were using the glue to sniff." Then, he said, "there was the nose problem" — players were gluing their racquets inside the sports hall in front of everybody. And soon there was an epidemic of nosebleeds, "even among umpires." The glue can also cause severe inflammation of the eyes. The ITTF had insisted that each hall where a championship match was held had to be equipped with a special gluing room, away from spectators, umpires, and tables. "Now we can breathe again in a sports arena."

But the ITTF couldn't ban glue entirely until a new method could be found of fixing the rubber to the racquet "without glue. We're close to finding the solution," he said, but he couldn't give me the details. It was some kind of secret.

The ITTF was also about to approve a heavier, larger ball, whose diameter would go from thirty-eight to forty millimeters. I'd already played with the "forty" ball, which seemed made for *defenseurs* like me. It looked funny the first time I saw it, like some children's toy. But this fat, floating ball gave me a much bigger target and more reaction time to take some of the sting out of my opponent's serve . . . and his attack.

Dr. Kahn didn't allow me to gloat. "The very best players will find a new system to play with the ball." A super Butterfly or Mark V that could turn the "forty" into a cannonball. But there were other benefits. World-class table tennis had been something of a flop as a spectator sport. "For the fans in a stadium, or on TV, the volleys are so fast, it was really impossible to follow the ball." The "forty" was much more visible. But would a fat ball alone turn ping-pong into a spectator sport? The game was too specialized. Ping-pong had been pared down to a basic text: serve and kill, serve and kill.

We were back to the topic of ping-pong and the aging process. "At the local level we can find people who could play up to eighty." But he wasn't quite convinced that seniors should be involved in competitive sports. "It's difficult to be sure that table tennis is safe for everyone . . . The chief problem after a certain age is heart strain. Ten people a year die at the table or a few hours after."

The stress and buildup of blood pressure might not be the best thing for men and women of seventy. Ping-pong, he said, "was a very complicated sport . . . There was a lot of hitting and a lot of standing still, and ping-pong was aerobic only part of the time," with a high stress on the cardiovascular system.

Here I was, at La Coupole, with the foremost doctor in the world devoted to table tennis, and I couldn't finish my salmon steak. I felt like a veteran of some mammoth, hundred-year war.

Philou was aging in front of my eyes . . . and Marty Reisman was like Don Quixote, going into battle with his hardbat at the age of sixty-nine. The Needle had had his cataracts removed and was flying to Vancouver to participate in the Tenth World Veterans Championship, held every two years for players over forty. I'd looked at the Vancouver Veterans' brochure, which was packed with information and hype: ping-pong had "the largest TV viewership in Asia of all sports during the 1996 Summer Olympics in Atlanta." Participants at previous Veterans' included former champions, like the Needle, and eighty-year-old men. It sounded like a fabulous jamboree, where players from all over the world could descend upon Vancouver, reminisce, and play. Dr. Kahn was totally against it.

"What does competition mean during a period of decreasing power? The body is a machine that you have to respect. When you're engaged in competition, you don't respect the machine."

"It's a meditative sport," I said. "It allows you to dream. Can't you dream at eighty? It's like being in a trance state."

"In a trance state," Dr. Kahn said, "you can't control everything. It could be dangerous for the body."

He liked the social aspects of the Veterans'— "It was a good reason to travel"—but not the tournament itself. "It's not necessary to win when we play for pleasure." But recreation wasn't what tournaments were about. They were filled with fury . . . and often with defeat.

I wondered what "recreation" he would recommend. "Cycling," he said. "Cycling and running," without competition. Dr. Kahn himself was a recreational runner; he ran every Sunday in the woods near his home.

I had a double scoop of coffee ice cream at La Coupole. I needed a strong hit of sugar. I couldn't console myself. The ITTF's very own medical maven was selecting bicycle wheels over ping-pong for Methuselahs like me. I looked at the emblem on my plate, that nude model with bobbed hair, Kiki of Montparnasse, who didn't flourish after les Années Folles: Kiki ended up starving in the streets. . . .

I RAN TO NEW YORK, played a little *ping* with my literary agent Georges Borchardt. Georges bears a spooky resemblance to actor Jean-Louis Barrault, who was so marvelous as the mime in Marcel Carné's *Children of Paradise* (1945). In fact, whenever I meet him, I feel that I'm in the presence of Baptiste, performing in whiteface on Paris' old Boulevard of Crime. But there were no ping-pong tables along that boulevard, or near Broadway, once the ping-pong capital of the world. "Baptiste" and I are locked out of Manhattan . . . until I discover a pool hall on Eighty-sixth Street that doubled as a ping-pong parlor. George is in his seventies, and I haven't noticed any slowing down; in fact, he was more ferocious and was giving me a harder and harder time at the table. I'd memorized most of Dr. Kahn's maxims: not only did we have to warm up and do stretching exercises before we played, but we also had to "cool down" after a match . . . and walk around after each game to work off the "isometric contractions." If we got tired in the middle

of a match, we had to stop, rest, drink some water and eat something to build up our sugar supply. I almost felt like a coach at INSEP, Dr. Kahn's disciple.

I had talked to other doctors, thanks to the Needle, who was like a dictionary of sources about ping-pong. Michael Scott, a dermatologist in Seattle, was also on the sports science committee of the ITTF and was like an Oliver Cromwell who uncovered which players were sniffing glue before a match. Dr. Scott was born in 1921 and not only still played ping-pong competitively, but was a "sixty-and-over champion." Unlike the master of Pitié-Salpêtriére, Scott believed that table tennis was "an ideal sport for the elderly, a life-time sport" that could be played by people of "seventy, eighty and over." It increases "hand-eye coordination, muscular activity, and keeps the skin healthy. It works on all activities of the skin . . . it keeps all joints active, fights against arthritis." Ping-pong, according to him, "was not excessively strenuous," but was "a steady, fast game" where each player had to "concentrate a hundred percent." And we both agreed that one of the great pleasures of the sport was that this concentration could often deliver a player into a kind of self-induced hypnosis that was somewhere between dreaming and waking. Most of us at the table, in the middle of fierce competition, had experienced "alpha," where we were outside our bodies in some mysterious, immortal land of the unknown. Dick Miles talks about this after one of his marathon matches with the Needle.

"Once I was playing Marty and all at once this wasn't me any longer. I might as well have been sitting there watching myself do things I had never imagined myself doing. I understood—I just knew—that I wasn't going to miss anymore. This thing took over; and both of us fell into sort of a trance. When it was over and he had lost, Marty came out of it and said to me, 'What happened? Where am I?'"

"Alpha" was a ping-pong player's paradise, where perfect harmony was achieved in the midst of battle, and mind and body moved in some mystical manner, and time itself seemed to bend to one's own will. This is what we longed for whenever we picked up a paddle, to get outside our skin, and enter into the dream of a game, where we were no longer self-conscious articles concerned about each individual stroke, where we danced without ambition or hunger to win, hypnotized by a little yellow ball. But what about when we danced to a much more mundane tune and were mere mortals trying to "read" the spin of an opponent's serve? "Regular physical activity" lent us "an alertness," Scott said.

Ping-pong was "a mental and physical equalizer," where a millionaire could meet across the table "with a man on welfare." It had lost its aristocratic roots, the private indoor gardens of royal tennis, where France's earlier Musketeers had played, Athos and Porthos.

"I don't feel I've slowed down," said Michael Scott. Wasn't that the illusion . . . and the wish of any active player? He was a seventy-nine-year-old man who looked fifty, according to the Needle. How could I tell? He had his own island in Puget Sound and invited me to visit. I imagined an island full of ping-pong players and wondered if I'd ever get there . . .

Dr. Joyce Ilson, a research scientist in the department of ophthalmology at Columbia, also agreed that ping-pong was one of the few games "one could play competitively at an older age." An expert on geriatric neurology, she felt that Methuselahs could grow younger on the table, sharpen their eyesight and their coordination, dance around a twenty year old. She wasn't talking about world-class competition. No eighty-year-old man could ever play Philou; and the former world champion and child prodigy of INSEP was beginning to struggle against the hardest hitting twenty-five year olds. World-class competition was an equation unto itself, where the slightest loss of speed was recorded on its own internal seismograph. The champions of classic ping-pong, like Lou Pagliaro and Johnny Leach, could compete well into their thirties, or into their forties perhaps, but they couldn't have survived the blitzkrieg that table tennis had become, where any loss of reaction time was fatal.

The Needle put me in touch with Dr. Steve Horowitz, chief of cardiology at Beth Israel Medical Center, and one of the hundred best players in America. I had to scramble to get him on the phone, between his practice at Beth Israel, his lectures, his teaching, and his tournament play. Steve was in his fifties, and his game was getting better and better. "The highest ranking in my life occurred this year." Like Joyce Ilson and Michael Scott, he believed in the "Methuselah syndrome," that an active player could remain active for a very long time. "We lose speed and strength much less than people think."

Ping-pong was a sport that embraced "a complete spectrum of aerobics," a sport where one was "completely engaged," and where "the body raced ahead of the mind." One had to play on "autopilot," in that curious fugue state "neurologically programmed below the thinking brain," where fluidity had to come out of chaos. If we had to *think*, we'd never be able to return a ball that was rocketing right at us. Ping-pong helped to "train that interesting and complex computer" of mind and body in a manner that was so much more "subtle than going to a health club." We both agreed that it was one of the purest forms of deep relaxation. Dr. Herbert Benson, author of *The Relaxation Response* (1975), a bestseller about meditative techniques, had been very much interested in table tennis as a form of "repetitive meditation." But the "drama of removing the sound of hard rubber" had impaired the meditative quality of ping-pong and had become "one of the most disturbing aspects to older players," players who had grown up on hard rubber and were completely frozen without the familiar pock of the ball.

Like Henry Miller, Georges Moustaki, Jean-François Kahn, and so many others of us, modern Tom Sawyers and Huckleberry Finns, Steve started to play around the time he was ten. He remembered being with his parents at a resort hotel, where he won a local tournament, and the very next morning his name was printed on each menu in the hotel dining room. His sudden fame got to Steve, and he realized that "this was my career," the cardiologist who plays serious ping-pong. He developed "an inherent passion" for a game whose skills, he feels, "go hand in hand with math . . . One of the best college teams in America is MIT." He considers Dick Miles a mathematical genius who had to "learn the mastery of all those angles and spins."

When Steve was still a kid he would play at Morris' club on West Seventy-third Street, which was a poor man's Marty Reisman's, a dungeonlike room in the basement of the Ansonia, a Beaux-Arts apartment-house castle that was built in 1904 and had once been the very best address in Manhattan. Caruso had lived there, Chaliapin, Toscanini, Babe Ruth; Flo Ziegfeld, father of the Ziegfeld Follies, kept an apartment for his wife and his mistresses. The Ansonia had once had the largest indoor swimming pool in the world and it was in a former closet attached to the pool that Morris' dungeon was situated. It did have one attraction: Dick Miles. Reisman's had Reisman and Morris had Dick Miles, who would arrive in a trenchcoat, looking like Humphrey Bogart. If Reisman was witty, open, gregarious, Dick Miles was completely closed. He would stand in his trenchcoat, chewing gum. But when he

played, he looked like a vulnerable little boy in short pants, who could chop and chop and chop. . . .

The first time Steve appeared at the Ansonia, he saw a woman sitting on a bench. "Sonny," she told him, "I'll play you a penny a point." She seemed very shopworn to Steve, who figured that he would make a killing. "She won about thirty thousand dollars in pennies" that she wouldn't collect.

"Who are you?" he growled, a terrific sore loser.

"Sonny," she said, "look at the name on your racquet."

He was clutching a Leah "Ping" Neuberger racquet in his hand, while he twitched in awe at "Ping," a former world mixed doubles champion. . . .

But we still hadn't talked about cardiology. Reisman, Miles, and "Dixie" Cartland were all patients of his. Dixie was eighty-five and played with a hematologist twice a week. Steve was something of a maverick among heart doctors. "Most cardiologists don't recommend competitive sports for heart patients." But the real problem was that his patients wouldn't stick to an exercise routine. "You need a hook. What's that hook gonna be?"

How could I answer? I wasn't a gerontologist, like Joyce Ilson. I was only a left-handed ping-pong player, struggling to survive in Paris' own little maze of tournaments. But after meeting with Dr. Kahn at La Coupole and feeling my own *mortality*, I called Steve Horowitz again. His nurse said I could have five minutes on the phone. I wanted to meet him face to face.

"Why?" he asked, looking at his watch, I imagined.

"It's a book," I said. "You can't really schmooze on the phone. Ping-pong . . . we're a brotherhood. And it's dying out."

The mournful tone in my voice must have swayed him.

"Meet me in an hour."

I grabbed my notebook and Mont Blanc pen and rushed to Beth Israel.

I was early for the interview. I sat in Steve's office, which looked out upon Stuyvesant Town, one of the very first middle-income housing projects put up in Manhattan, right after the war. Social philosopher and urbanist Lewis Mumford had decried it, calling Stuyvesant Town's thirty-five towers the paraphernalia of a police state. But Mumford was wrong. Like most futurologists, he couldn't predict the future better than a blind child. An *atmosphere* had grown around Stuyvesant Town, thick with trees and vines and tall grass that created its own variable environment.

Steve entered his office with a bag of apples, the perfect ammunition of a heart doctor. He'd been at a banquet the night before where the lecturer was Frank O. Gehry, the most visible architect on the planet after putting up the Guggenheim Museum in Bilbao. What would Mumford have made of it? Gehry had seized a sleepy Basque town full of widows in black shawls and turned it into a metropolis with the magic of *one* museum.

He'd talked about the creative process at his lecture. "If you asked me to design a shopping mall," Gehry said, "I wouldn't have a clue." Gehry needed to build "by pushing against something," by destroying old boundaries. And Steve had to destroy the old boundaries and shibboleths on aging. "We need a new attitude about the aging process. One ages because you physically can't do anything. Very few middle-aged people engage in good physical exercise. Of people who've suffered a heart attack, only fifteen percent do some form of rehabilitation . . . after five years it's down to three percent."

Steve wasn't very optimistic about Dr. Kahn's plan of cycling for seniors. "People are uninterested in pumping a bicycle pedal if you're going nowhere . . . you can't use a bicycle in the city. With all the traffic, you wouldn't have a chance.

"I totally acknowledge that competitive exercise has dangers . . . but it also has benefits. Can competitive fire get people into trouble? Yes. Particularly for the proverbial weekend athlete. If I could offer a schema, it would be that it's better to get people involved. One of the biggest problems of the geriatric age is depression."

That was the real devil. Once people withdrew and fell into a deep melancholia, it was hard to revive them, to bring them back into the daily routines of the world. Hemingway, who was a depressive all his life, understood this. He died of melancholy, shot himself when his body and mind failed him, when he could no longer write or enjoy the most simple pleasures. He'd mentioned this to a young journalist, Lillian Ross, years before his suicide. It was 1949. Papa was approaching fifty. He was on his way to Europe, and he'd stopped in Manhattan to see his editor and go to a couple of boxing matches. Papa adored boxing and hated New York, a city of "publishers and parasites." Papa was always on the move—it masked his melancholy—and he worried what would happen if he ever stood still and lost his interest in prize fights. "If you ever quit going for too long a time, then you never go near them. That would be too dangerous . . . finally, you end up in one room and won't move."

And this was the most disturbing disease of old age—mental and physical paralysis, the very fear of being alive. Any kind of exercise could help counter this, particularly ping-pong. "Competition," Steve said, "has a symbolic meaning. It pushes back demons . . . makes people feel young again. The most enthusiastic people at the U.S. Opens are the older players. There was a Filipino guy in his nineties who kept talking about his rating. . . ."

Steve wasn't really arguing with Dr. Kahn's premise. He realized that competitive sports for older people could pose a risk. But, he said, most people had heart attacks while they were watching television, not while they were engaged in a sport. "It's an easy cop-out to tell everyone at risk not to do this, that, and everything." Ping-pong was good for the psyche and the soul. "The reality of practice makes people human. People like to take risks. It resurrects them, the meaning of their lives changes." It was important to "stay socially engaged, physically active." Otherwise one ended up in Hemingway's room, a psychic suicide.

Steve made a distinction between the art of medicine and the science of medicine. "The science of medicine tells people not to do things." It was cautious and correct. "The art of medicine tries to make things work for human beings . . . it makes compromises and takes chances. If you accept certain limits and only work within them, your only existence is an envelope that gradually closes," like Hemingway's room.

Dr. Kahn, he said, who'd helped patch up champions like Philou, "was dealing with an elite. Everyone looks bad compared to them . . . yes, you'll fall out of the top ten in world-class competition as your skill declines." But he wasn't going to mourn France's Musketeers. "Most people go through their lives without realizing their potential." They gradually lose their perspective and sink into their own personal oblivion.

Steve was totally passionate about the healing aspects of table tennis. Even with age, he said, "we can increase muscle strength." He talked about a West Indian *pongiste*, George Brathwaite, who was in his late sixties "but looked like a thirty-five-year-old Olympic athlete." I remembered him from Reisman's more than thirty years ago, not so much because of his particular attack, but the wonder of his smile, which was beyond manner or stealth, had no hidden motive. And it was while playing George that an "epiphany" came to Steve. "This is how we're all supposed to look at sixty-seven!" Seniors "subjected to aerobic training can substantially produce muscle, increase speed and balance" and prevent themselves from tripping all over the place. But few of them, I had to admit, had the grace and good will of George Brathwaite.

Still, old or young, the strange music of practicing at a table and tumbling into the rhythm of a game could give one a "feeling of immortality, of total well-being." That was the reward of serious, steady ping-pong. "Vigorous exercise (is) only a risk to people who are not used to exercise."

But Steve was a cardiologist, after all. And like Dr. Kahn, he believed that anyone who played competitively should have an electrocardiogram, a stress test, and perhaps a PET (position emission tomography) scan, a three-dimensional imaging of the heart. But he wasn't about to abandon healthy Methuselahs to a bicycle wheel, like Sisyphus condemned to eternal labor, rolling and rolling his stone.

I left Steve to his own Sisyphean labor as a heart specialist and crossed Stuyvesant Square. There was a curious statue in magnificent darkened bronze of old peg-legged Peter Stuyvesant, the tyrannical governor general of New Amsterdam (as New York had been called under the Dutch). The square itself had once belonged to Pegleg Pete, had been a small parcel of his property. He was a terrible son of a bitch, a racist, without much pity. But modern New York, with all its contradictions, grew out of his stubborn, autocratic rule. Old Pete bent to no one. He was holding a staff, as was his wont—how could he knock his subjects over the head without one? He had two rows of buttons on his jacket and a bow on his single shoe. He was wearing a skullcap, like a wizard or a wise man. But the deep bronze gave him the aura of a *métèque*; he was one of us, a vagabond and a voyager . . . with the enormous hands of a basketball player, my spiritual dad, Pegleg Pete.

I continued toward Union Square, which had been gussied up since my childhood, when Klein's department store, with its endless rows of merchandise, dominated the entire southeast section of the square; now it was cluttered with boutiques and ice cream shops. I devoured an enormous cup of Cappuccino Commotion at the local Häagen-Dazs, unable to reconcile my Hamletlike hesitations, the different voices in my head. I'm sure that the good Doctors Kahn and Horowitz were both correct. To play or not to play, that was the question. I'd rather go bumping into the night, armed with my picot, play a young killer under the Périphérique, than sit like some victim of self-paralysis, gathering dust in Hemingway's room. . . .

SEVEN

The Chiseler King

I HAVE A CONFESSION TO make. I wasn't always faithful to Marty Reisman when he ruled the Upper West Side as the last great ping-pong impresario of the 1970s. When I didn't feel like trekking up to Ninety-sixth Street, I would stop off at Morris' dump in the Ansonia's bowels, with scraps of light shimmering off the swimming pool that was Morris' next-door neighbor. It was the habitat of retired stockbrokers, who would babble about their most current kill on the Big Board. They would sit in their locker room wearing goggles and nose plugs, like mariners who'd just escaped from the sea while the rest of us toiled in Morris's dungeon, hot as the Sahara in summer and winter. But it was worth that maddening heat to watch Dick Miles play. He was the sphinx of American ping-pong, so tight-mouthed that I never saw him smile or whisper a word of hello. I was infinitesimal, outside that tiny orbit of whoever he deigned to look upon. No one seemed to exist for Miles, not even the partner he played with. He communed one-on-one with the ping-pong ball, and it was this ferocious concentration that made him impossible to beat. He'd dominated the game in the forties and fifties, winning the U.S. Open ten times, though he'd never been a world singles champion or won the British Open, like the Needle. Did he also lack that killer instinct? "If you want to be a great player, you have to be angry if you lose. I myself used to get very sad if I lost."

Miles was an *isolato* who carried Joyce's *Ulysses* under his arm wherever he went. If Reisman was half clown, an honorary Globetrotter, a born entertainer and magician, Miles didn't care to entertain.

He would chop away at you until little was left of your body and soul.

He was like Reisman's inverted double. If the Needle was strictly a downtown brat, Miles was born on the Upper West Side in 1925 and had his own chaotic family life. His dad wasn't a gambler, like Reisman's. He simply disappeared from the household when Miles was two. And Miles lived with his mother, his uncle, and his maternal grandparents. He started to play miniature ping-pong with his uncle on the dining room table when he was nine or ten, and discovered how to hit the ball "square to the line of flight," as if he were practicing some higher form of mathematics inside his head. There was already something mythic about the man who claimed that "he owed his singular table tennis chop defense to hours and hours of Chinese handball where you had to learn to slice the ball into the right pavement-block," according to Tim Boggan.

"In the late 30s, early 40s, it was possible to find as many as 1-2-3-4 table tennis clubs located up and down Broadway from Fifty-fourth to Ninety-sixth Streets," when Manhattan itself was a ping-pong emporium.

Miles worked his way from club to club until he drifted into Lawrence's, with all its lore about Legs Diamond. He was fourteen, a duffer and a "debutante," who already understood the art and science of ping-pong. He quit school, would sleep well into the afternoon, and then put in an eleven-hour day at Lawrence's. His grandmother soon caught onto his tricks. She'd lock him out of the family apartment, and the young apprentice would stand out in the hall wailing until someone let him in, while his grandmother screamed, "You're a bum."

By 1942 the bum was ranked seventh in the U.S. He had a heart murmur and sat out the war. But he still toured the country, giving exhibitions to soldiers and sailors. Rubber racquets and fresh ping-pong balls were hard to find, and there were fewer and fewer tournaments on account of travel restrictions and gas rationing.

It was in Detroit at the '45 Nationals that the bum finally "arrived." He was nineteen. "I was playing in my first National final, was a skinny 111 pounds, and had a big nose." But he won, and Graham Steenhoven, president of the Michigan Table Tennis Association, who never had much love for Lawrence's New York band of players, presented him with the trophy and said, "Here, I hope you *behave* like a champion."

That November, at the New York City Open, Dixie Cartland, who'd just returned from the war, beat Miles in five games. "I literally cried on losing. I told a girlfriend I'd lost to a man 30 years old. He seemed like the oldest man in the world."

But at the '46 Nationals, held in Manhattan, Miles completely clobbered the field, losing only one game during the entire tournament. He was, according to *Table Tennis Topics*, "in a class by himself," number one in the land, and already canonized by a plurality of USTTA members as the greatest U.S. men's singles player "of all times" (competitive ping-pong was less than thirty years old).

Miles was considered America's favorite son to win the men's singles at the '47 World's in Paris, but he lost in the first round to Britain's Johnny Leach. And though he would continue to dominate U.S. table tennis, he would never reach the finals at any future world championship. It was as if Miles' own mythology had crumpled up inside himself, and he would remain an enigma who suffered some kind of stage fright during world-class competition. The Needle was much more erratic, often clowning in the middle of an important match, perhaps to hide his own hunger to win. But Miles had the icy ruthlessness of a champion . . . and a nearly perfect game. He was a human metronome who could wear down any opponent with his relentless clockwork. But he still couldn't beat Johnny Leach.

I HAD MY OWN CURIOUS ping-pong with Miles in the spring of 2000. I wanted to meet him. The Needle had given me his number. There was a lifetime love-hate between them, the yin and yang of American ping-pong—one cold, dark, introspective; the other warm, funny, willing to lend you his last hat and coat. Reisman had been grudgingly respectful of Miles in *The Money Player*. "Dick Miles was an unusual fellow. He was four years older than I, cool and distant, and not at all popular with the people who frequented Lawrence's. Players would come to him for advice and he would stare through them as if he had not heard, or simply look away. When he ran into someone from Lawrence's on social occasions elsewhere he would pretend not to know him . . .

"A man who knew him said that if they spent two years planning to burglarize a mansion, Miles would get inside the mansion, begin socializing with the hosts, and forget who his fellow robbers were.

"But Dick Miles could play table tennis. . . ."

Miles had never been the mentor that Marty would have liked to have, but Miles had mentored no one. He was too absorbed in his own internal clock. He ignored Marty, wouldn't even recognize him at Lawrence's, but he would admit that Marty "got good very, very fast."

Miles had stopped playing. He had a blind spot in one eye and a damaged heart. And he wouldn't meet with me no matter how hard I cajoled. "Talk to Tim Boggan," he said. "Tim knows more about me than I do. He remembers every match I played." Ah, but I wanted to hear about Miles right from the horse's mouth. He would only answer written questions.

"Do you have a fax machine?"

I felt like a schoolboy, but I faxed him eight questions, the first of which was "what's the most painful memory you have about ping-pong?"

He mentioned that "disaster" in 1947.

"I'd reached my peak in 1944-45, won my first U.S. Open right after the war. But the world championships didn't resume until 1947. It was in Paris at the Palais des Sports. I was very nervous. It was my first round singles match with Johnny Leach. The matches had been going on for five days. I'd beaten him during the team competition (for the Swaythling Cup). But when I played him in the singles, I didn't get any kind of warm-up. It was cold in the stadium. You could see your breath. I choked . . . my arm froze. I couldn't hold the racquet. My wrist cramped. I lost in three straight (games) . . .

"For the next seven years I had to change my style completely. Earlier I would either attack or defend. If my opponent decided to attack, I would play defense . . . I could always adapt. Now I had to worry about that cramp in my arm. I was afraid to play long points. I was under a handicap. I had to counterattack. . . .

"I was playing Vana (at the '48 World's in London's Wembley Stadium). I was ahead 16-9 in the deciding game. I blew it, I blew the game. Next year in Sweden, I lost to Leach again, 26-24, in the fifth game (of the quarterfinals). . . ."

But there was a deeper tale to tell. The cruel dance between winner and loser in any sport. Miles *had* to win against Johnny Leach at the '47 World's, but he didn't. That match traumatized him. Blame it

on a cramp. But he couldn't overcome that loss to Leach, who would go on to win two world championships. And America's most consistent, dangerous player, with flawless strokes and a mean, mathematical gaze that could read the most devilish spin— "his eyes look as though they had spent the afternoon inspecting the interiors of watches," Murray Kempton wrote about him—who should have been a world champion, remained a kind of elegant, brooding invisible man.[1]

But unlike Reisman, Miles was one of the few world-class players of the classic era who made the switch from hard rubber to sponge. And I asked him about the switch. "I felt more comfortable with sponge against spongers," he said on the phone. "But I didn't have a big spinning game. I learned to play defensive with sponge. I was beating players I couldn't beat with hard rubber."

I asked him about the often repeated rumor that he never went to Lawrence's without *Ulysses* under his arm. I could hear him laugh. "*Ulysses* is still under my arm. I've only read it about fifty times. I've been reading that book all my life."

And was there any relationship between writing and ping-pong?

"They're both very hard," he said. I would have loved to ask him if words themselves had any spin. But I had to hold to the little script I'd prepared.

What about Lawrence's, how had America's first and last "ping-pong college" developed his game?

"It was the hub and the nucleus, the place where players could climb on each other's back." Miles had climbed on the backs of Sol Schiff and

---

1 Miles did win the mixed doubles at Wembley in 1948 with Thelma Thall, but he was so scornful of this event that he arrived at the table for one of the matches wearing gloves and an overcoat.

Lou Pagliaro, who were in their prime when he began appearing at Lawrence's. "All sports have certain places," he said. And if Schiff had lived in Chicago, then Chicago might have become the mecca of ping-pong.. Miles remembered when it cost "sixty cents an hour to play, and the players rebelled when it went up to sixty-five . . . no one had money in those days."

"There were forty-six homicides a year in New York," and now there might be five in a single night. "We played until five in the morning then ate at the House of Chan, and I'd go with Marty to shoot a little pool."

But he didn't feel there was any particular ping-pong culture in the classic era. "New York was a different place. I used to take girls to Central Park in the forties, and sometimes I slept in the park."

But New York itself hadn't shaped his game. Lawrence's could have been anywhere. I would have liked to wrestle with Miles a bit. It was no accident that Bobby Fischer had "trained" at the Marshall Chess Club in Manhattan, or that Miles and the Needle had both "gone to college" at Lawrence's. New York had once been the land of luftmenschen, where people could live on air, feed themselves for nickels at any Automat, and thrive in a nighttime world of sports and games, remove themselves from Manhattan's moneyed song, the constant, grinding search for wealth. . . . Ping-pong was a kind of fierce *no* to the dominant culture: the sheer force of play was much more vital and *thrilling* than any career.

I asked him about Reisman, always a touchy topic to Miles. "Marty was a great player, probably the most colorful player. He had the great forehand," and so did Miles. "People don't think of me as a freehand attacker." But when the American *pongistes* descended upon Europe after the war, "Marty and me were demolishing players." People began to say that "the American style was ruining

table tennis. Ivor Montagu"—president of the ITTF—"considered raising the net from six inches back to six and three quarters." But the Americans lost to the Czechs in team play, and the net was never raised again.

I felt like a wily serpent, waiting, waiting to spring on Miles, but he wouldn't depart from my script. He'd visited China in '71, had played an exhibition match in Peking, yet refused to talk about the trip, or about his personal life. He had written two articles on ping-pong for *Sports Illustrated* and was quite proud that one of the articles had appeared in the same anthology with William Faulkner.

I didn't know what to expect. It's Reisman who told me that Miles had been a journalist and was also writing fiction.

But the two pieces, which had appeared in 1965 and 1966, startled me. They were the very best things I'd ever read about ping-pong. They reminded me a bit of Louise Brooks, the invisible actress, whose one short book, *Lulu in Hollywood*, was so much more incisive than the sickening, false memoirs of movie stars and the enormous tomes of film historians. Lulu had been right *there*. "Staring down at my name in lights on the marquee of the Wilshire Theatre was like reading an advertisement of my own isolation."

Miles had the same tickets of isolation. He'd also been *there*, in the center of the storm . . . as a pong-pong player. Lawrence's, he writes, "served for 20 golden years as an incubator of U.S. champions and finishing school for hustlers, but I remember it most vividly as an outpatient refuge for the unlikeliest assortment of oddballs west of Creedmoor (a notorious state mental institution). It was, I recall, a kind of USO for weirdies—a home away from home." The proprietor, Herwald Lawrence, was "a lofty West Indian with an impeccable British accent. From his desk near the windows fronting Broadway his imperial voice blasted through a hand micro-phone and policed the reaches of the establishment . . . . 'We do not tolerate banging rackets upon the tables, gentlemen! . . . On table No. 7, please, not so loudly there, old top.'"

Miles describes his first appearance at Lawrence's as a raw youth. Unable to find the club, he happened to look up and saw someone near an open window hurl "his racket and one sneaker at his opponent (who ducked) and the familiar items fell at my feet two stories below on the sidewalk. 'This must be the place' I reasoned."

And like some D'Artagnan searching for his own land of musketeers, he climbed up Lawrence's rickety stairs. "One look made it clear to me that I had never played the game. All around wild men were climbing walls to return seemingly impossible smashes. At one table the then U.S. champion, Louis Pagliaro, a 5-foot-2, 100 pound wisp, was imitating a comet. At another I saw Douglas Cartland, also a star, topspin a dozen successive forehand drives into the chop of a stubborn defensive artist. Agony contorted Cartland's face at every stroke. Finally, trying for the kill, Cartland missed, and with an anguished cry he lifted his foot right onto the table and in a spasm of overwhelming grief began clawing at his trouser leg until the cloth parted in tatters."

He describes the look of one particular Lawrence habitué, Hugo Batzlinger, whose "face had the faintly bluish hue and the translucency of skimmed milk—a Ping-Pong parlor pallor." Batzlinger was a total fanatic. "To improve his back-hand he tried self-hypnosis, but he put himself into such a deep trance one day that he lost a game 21-0." Hugo would attack, attack, attack, but his "kill shot" always failed him. He had the *elbow*. "Sometimes known as the 'apple.' He was a lumper, a choker. On clutch points Hugo was merely a flurry of mismated limbs, an epileptic dervish with one enormous elbow."

In "Spongers Seldom Chisel," Miles writes about the mythical long point between Poland's Alex Ehrlich, King of the Chiselers, and Romania's Paneth Farcas, during the team championships at the 1936 World's in Prague. (In ping-pong parlance, a chiseler is a monomaniacal defensive player who will never, never attack, and keeps pushing the ball until he can no longer stand on his feet). The first point of their match lasted two hours and twelve minutes. Ehrlich had his special, outsized "chiseling bat." He was determined to wear Farcas down at the very beginning of the game. He pushed and pushed, and after seventy minutes the score was still 0-0, but Farcas "had shriveled with every return and now looked like a hunchbacked robot." Ehrlich himself was suffering. "The extra weight of his chiseling bat had begun to tire his arm," so he "deftly switched his bat and continued the point left-handed." But there was a problem with the umpire. After eighty-five minutes his neck had locked into one position, and a new umpire had to be called in.

The arena began to empty. Ehrlich didn't care. To keep himself relaxed, he had a chessboard put on a table near the sideline and would whisper his moves to the Polish team captain. Meanwhile the ball "had crossed the net more than twelve thousand times," according to the Chiseler King. But after two hours, Farcas' arm began to freeze. And he lost the first point.

Twenty minutes into the second point, a member of Ehrlich's team reached into his equipment bag "and pulled out a knife, a long loaf of bread and a two-foot Polish sausage." Thinking that the Poles "were prepared for a winter siege," Farcas started to attack. When Ehrlich returned the ball twice, Farcas, in a fit, "sent the ball and bat together sailing wildly over the King's head," and "ran screaming off the court."

In response to Ehrlich's long point, the ITTF decided to "invigorate" the sport of ping-pong. It decreed that a game had to stop after twenty minutes, the victory going to whoever was ahead. To encourage much livelier play it lowered the net from six and three-quarter inches to six, and helped create attacking champions, like Bohumil Vana ("the Bouncing Czech"), Marty Reisman, and Miles himself. And the heart of classic ping-pong came from matches between attackers and defenders such as Bergmann and Leach, "those incredible ballet dancers who ranged from 15 feet behind the table." In one match, Bergmann "charged in for a drop shot with such momentum that to avoid crashing into the table he leaped on it, bounded across the net, and there brandished his arms like King Kong while he glanced menacingly at his opponent."

LIKE LULU HERSELF, LOUISE BROOKS, Miles has a marvelous eye for detail. He describes the Needle at London's Empire Pool in 1948, as "a tall, cadaverous New Yorker with a bird's face and black-rimmed glasses. His only muscle is an overdeveloped biceps. Nevertheless, his forehand drive was the most explosive shot in the game."

Miles also wrote a primer, a practice book, but one can only wish that he'd ranged much deeper, used his wizard's touch to articulate the metaphysics of ping-pong. He doesn't have much appetite for the *pongistes* of today.

"To the unaccustomed eye a topflight modern table tennis match might well appear a game played in the recreation room of an asylum by two berserk patients." Yet that asylum is all we have. Modern ping-pong is much closer to the chaos that surrounds us, a clipped, bewildering language that has no room for chiseler kings. . . .

Photos

Reisman (left) and Miles (right), America's two great warriors, posing at a recent national championship, without the bitterness and pain of their lifelong rivalry: the two champions first played against each other more than fifty-five years ago.

Table Tennis's First King: Victor Barna of Hungary, five-time world singles champion, who had the deadliest backhand drive in the game.

Michel Glikman, the young French champion who could no longer represent France, circa 1932.

Raymond Verger, Michel Glikman's bête noir, who drove him out of competition in France.

Life on the Lower East Side: Marty Reisman, at three, with his big brother, David, at five, in Seward Park, 1933. It's David who might have been the champion if Marty hadn't "bumped" him out of the way. Their childhood reads like a Dickensian fairy tale.

Ruth Aarons, circa 1936.

Dick Miles (top row, center) with several of his classmates, graduating from the eighth grade in January 1940.

A rare photograph of young Reisman at Lawrence's, in 1944, practicing his backhand chop. "No one club in the world could ever lay claim to being the home of such a huge assemblage" of players "who managed to achieve world class status without the existence of a single coach or the benefit of a single moment of coaching," writes Marty Reisman.

Reisman and Miles are featured on a poster during a 1949 "championship tour."

Innocence Abroad: Marty in London, 1949, preparing for his championship match at Wembley Stadium.

Dick Miles at Lawrence's, once a speakeasy owned by Legs Diamond. The mythic bullet holes behind table seven were souvenirs from the time when Jack Diamond "was shot at and his magic legs danced him out of harm's way," according to Reisman.

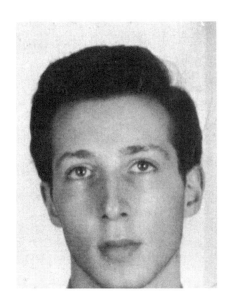

Portrait of the Artist as a Young Man: Marty, in 1950, a year after he won the British Open.

Reisman at the height of his career–ranked number three in the world.

Venice, 1952: Reisman, the wandering ping-pong knight, feeds a pigeon in San Marco Square.

Bombay, 1952: Reisman signs his autograph just before Hiroji Satoh conquered the world and utterly destroyed classic table tennis.

Osaka, 1952: Dixie Cartland (bottom row, ninth from the left) with Reisman and reigning world singles champion Hiroji Satoh (bottom row, sixth from the left) during an exhibition match. Reisman would win his match against Satoh and Satoh's revolutionary sponge rubber bat. But that victory was one more element of his quixotic life: not even a magician like Marty could uncrown Satoh in a non-championship match.

Dick Miles, with his racquet in his pocket, after defeating Richard Bergmann at one of the U.S. Opens, somewhere in the 1950s.

5 TIMES WORLD CHAMPION — RICHARD BERGMANN (ENGLAND)

Richard Bergmann, the most dynamic, colorful player who ever lived. Bergmann would jump right onto the table if he had to, or tumble into another room to retrieve an errant ball. The caption attached to the photograph belies the fact that Bergmann was world champion only four times, for Austria in 1937, and for England in 1939, 1948, and 1950; he probably would have won his elusive fifth title had it not been for the war.

Reisman and Dixie Cartland in 1953, during one of their whirlwind tours; we find them in Cairo with President Mohammed Naguib of Egypt, who seems omnipotent behind his cluttered desk.

The Needle looking like a matador.

Reisman with one of his Hock hard rubber bats, playing the dapper shark in polka-dotted pants at his club during the 1960s. The clock above his left shoulder reads 4:34 PM, just about the time Reisman would usually arrive.

The Two Masters at Play: Marty and Dick Miles at Reisman's Broadway club, 1964.

Young John Tannehill receives his first check as a ping-pong player from Marty Reisman at a tournament during the 1960s.

Tannehill, in glasses and overalls, with the rest of the U.S. team, leaving one of the buildings at Ching Hua University, near Peking.

Three-time World Singles Champion Chuang Tse-tung, whom most aficionados consider the best all-around player who ever lived, during a championship match, circa 1965. Chuang might have gone on to win two or three other singles championships if Chairman Mao hadn't pulled all his players out of world competition during China's Cultural Revolution.

Dick Miles with superstar Chuang Tse-tung on the Great Wall of China.

Ping-Pong Diplomacy: Premier Chou poses with Graham Steenhoven (at his left) and the American team (note: author and *pongiste* Tim Boggan is third from the left, bottom row).

Dick Miles with Premier Chou En-lai in Peking.

U.S. and Chinese teams at Peking Stadium, Spring 1971.

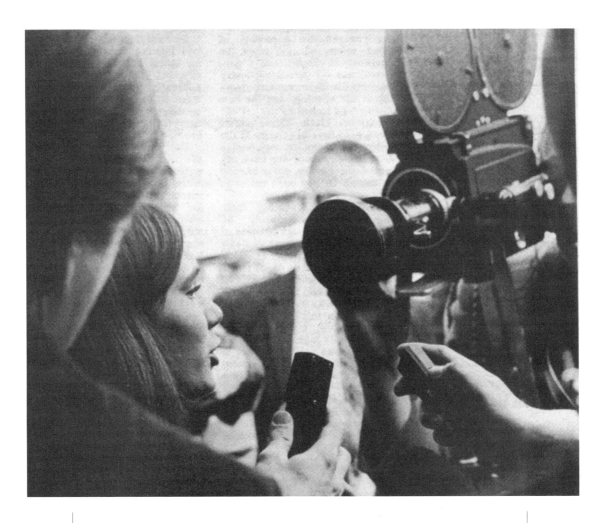

15-year-old Judy Bochenski being interviewed on her return from China in 1971.

The Horse Whisperer of Paris: Michel Courteaux, at Vincennes with Rita Royale II in 1982.

My coach, Jean-Louis Fleury, during one of our training sessions.

Pierre Zang at seventy-five, still one of the fiercest competitors on the allée Verte.

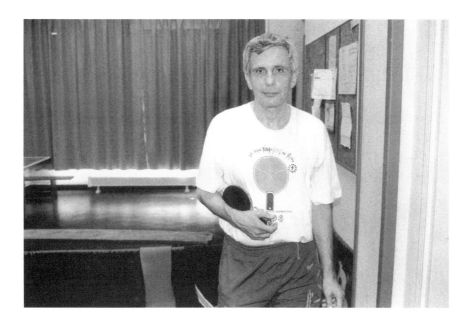

The author, with his picot, at the allée Verte, wearing a T-shirt that was made especially for him and Georges Moustaki to advertise an exhibition match in Gijón, Spain, when the two musketeers of U.S. Metro were trounced by the musketeers of Spain.

Moustaki playing on the allée Verte.

David and Goliath: Chuang Tse-tung and USTTA president Graham Steenhoven in a 1972 "Ping-Pong Diplomacy" exhibition in Detroit.

One of the epic duels between Reisman and Miles in the old Madison Square Garden.

The Left-Handed Gun

I WAS HAVING DINNER AT La Rotonde, in the heart of Hemingwayland, when I drank a prodigious amount of beer. I stumbled down the winding stairs to La Rotonde's tiny toilet and soon discovered that I'd locked myself in. It was the fate of left-handers in a right-handed world. My right hand wasn't strong enough to untwist the lock, and I couldn't grasp the bolt properly with my left. I panicked, of course, imagined spending my whole life in La Rotonde's toilet, without ping-pong, books, or beer. . . .

I started to scream and curse. A waiter arrived, managed to calm me, *and* open the door by digging at the lock with a knife. I shoved fifty francs into his right hand, but he wouldn't accept any largesse. It was La Rotonde's privilege, he said, to extricate gentlemen from its own deep well.

This wasn't my first or last contretemps. I was constantly bumping and banging into people, blaming myself. I'd had nervous fits since I was a child, worried about everything, and didn't know why. And then I happened upon *The Left-Handed Syndrome*, a controversial book by a right-handed Canadian psychologist, Stanley Coren. Coren had become the bane of left-handers because of his book. Some left-handers, he said, "may be pathological." And most left-handers were disappearing from the population much faster than right-handers. "For groups aged 80 and older, less than 1 percent of the population is left-handed. . . . Left-handedness can cost a man 10 years and 1 month in terms of life expectancy."

I was beginning to feel more and more like an invalid and a pariah, yet the book was strangely soothing. It was telling me who the hell I am.

Left-handedness has always been the mark of the devil. There wasn't a single word in any language that had a kind thing to say about us. *Left* comes from the Anglo-Saxon *lyft*, the word for "weak" or "broken." *Gauche* in French can also mean "clumsy" and "uncouth." In Italian *mancino* comes from *mancus*, something that is "crooked" or "maimed." And in Latin, *sinister* is derived from *sinistrum*, or evil. *Levja*, or left-handed in Russian, is considered an insult. And in Romany, *bongo* can "describe a crooked card game, a fixed horse race, or a wicked and dishonest person."

We can't seem to win.

During the Middle Ages, whenever witches were examined, a mole on the left side of the body was a sure sign of the devil. Among the Eskimos, lefties are shunned as sorcerers and demons. In Morocco they're *s'ga*, or wicked as the devil. And for the ancient Hebrews, all pure people had to guard against the temptation of *yezer-ha-ra*, "the angel on the left."

I'd never realized that my poor left hand symbolized so much wickedness. But there were certain compensations. Because of our rarity (10 percent of the population worldwide), we excelled in particular sports, like baseball, boxing, fencing . . . and ping-pong. There were simple and complicated reasons for this. *Handedness* was only one part of our anatomical picture. People were also right-or left-sided, which included "footedness, eyedness, and earedness." In baseball, some of the greatest sluggers, such as Babe Ruth and Ted Williams, had *"crossed hand-eye sideness."* That is, they were left-handed and right-eyed. Babe Ruth was a particular paradox. Having grown up in an orphanage (even though his father, who kept a saloon, was still alive), he was taught by the Catholic brothers at St. Mary's to scribble with his right hand. Yet he was a left-handed pitcher and a home run king. And Coren was able to track down a photograph of the Babe "looking through a telescope with his right eye." This would have been a real advantage at home plate, since a left-handed batter *faces* the pitcher with his right eye.

In boxing the advantages of a left-hander are obvious. A southpaw's punches seem to come out of nowhere, since a typical right-hander can't defend against a fighting stance with such atypical angles.

In fencing the advantage is even greater. In 1980, 48 percent of the world's top twenty-five fencers were all left-handed. A southpaw's unorthodox "angles of attack" gave him the power of surprise. Suddenly the right-hander was caught in an unfamiliar world.

The same was true for ping-pong. Right-handers weren't used to encountering a left-handed smash. This was one reason why Philou was so devastating. His attack would rocket out of unfamiliar territory, and no one in world-class competition had an extra nanosecond to adjust to his game.

I'm only a little leaguer, but the advantage I had was also surprise. Right-handers had to face a left-handed picot. My ball has a wicked hop and a crazy spin, and when they tried to attack it, the ball usually went into the net or bounded off the table. Of course, when *I* played a left-hander, I had the same problem of unfamiliarity. And if I couldn't adjust, it was my ball that sank into the net.

But there were more subtle, darker reasons for my winning scores against right-handers. I had a devilish concentration. If an opponent was ahead 20-12, one point from victory, and if he grew overconfident and started to sleep at the table, I could climb on his back, chip away at the score, until it was much too late.

I also had an "asocial" aggressiveness, a desire to win at any cost. The game meant too much. It wasn't local competition, a little league, it was a much larger arena, as if my very existence were at stake. I was a left-handed gun, with a rage that was like a self-inflicted wound. I would never have thrown racquet or ball at my opponent, but I could have, would have, killed him in my dreams.

Yet I was scared to death at the beginning of a match. And I developed nyctophobia—a fear of night—only on the nights I had to play. I could barely leave my apartment. Suddenly Paris was a bewildering place. I couldn't tell one Metro line from the next. And when I rambled around in some poor man's zone of the ninth arrondissement, it would take me half an hour to find the other team's club, even if it was a block away from the Metro. I'd walk in tightening circles, carrying an umbrella, like Batman's private devil, the Penguin (if my memory of comics hasn't failed me), and in some terrific daze, I'd arrive at the right gym.

And who am I, the left-handed chronicler of ping-pong, to blame Dick Miles for losing that match to Johnny Leach at the Palais des Sports? I would have peed in my pants, had a frozen elbow and wrist, gone temporarily blind. I always lost my first match, unless Jean-Louis was there to shake that nyctophobia out of my soul and bring me back into the land of light. . . .

Naturally I had to find the proper goat. I blamed my childhood, likened myself to Miles and the Needle. I'd dueled constantly with my dad, a right-hander who make fun of my odd, stubborn ways. He couldn't understand my love of books. I'd started reading late, but when I'd finally "captured" the alphabet, I didn't want to let go. Words had their own picture on the page, like clusters of big and little boats on the unvarying waves of a white sea. I remember my first bookcase, because I had to beg for the right and privilege of having one. It was more precious than any Phi Beta Kappa key or medal from some minister. It was where I housed my books, those cheap Modern Library editions of Dostoyevsky, Tolstoy, St. Augustine, Pascal—that was my home amid the chaos of my father's constant attacks. I was Raskolnikov, Dick Diver, and Anna Karenina, partnering their own terrible isolation. And when poor Dick floats from hamlet to hamlet, each one a little more obscure, in the finale of *Tender Is the Night*, I understood that closing down. He was a symbolic left-hander in a right-handed world. There was no place for Dick Diver.

But it wasn't until I read Coren's book that I realized that at least *some* of my predicament was outside psychology. Coren believes that "right-handedness is a *genetically* fixed trait." Southpaws are some kind of freak; few of us were ever meant to be. "Perhaps left-handedness should be looked upon as a failure to reach right-handedness." But why did this failure come about and what does it mean? According to some researchers, left-handedness is a permanent disability—a neurological disease—caused by birth-related trauma and stress. And males are easy targets. "When it comes to birth complications, males are much more vulnerable to neurological damage than are females." And it gets worse. We produce an overabundance of schizophrenics and criminals. John Dillinger, Jack the Ripper, Billy the Kid, John Wesley Hardin, and the Boston Strangler (Albert Henry DeSalvo) were all southpaws. Arthur Penn deals with this singularity in his portrait of Billy the Kid, *The Left-Handed Gun* (1958), an odd and brooding film, unlike any Western you're ever bound to see. The Kid, as played by Paul Newman, is utterly unpredictable, as likely to dance with a broom as kill a man. He's word-blind. Words on a page are all

"twisted-up." Billy can only *read* with a gun. He's hysterical half the time, like a traumatized child. The camera itself is schizophrenic, wanders everywhere, forcing us to blink. Penn is another right-hander with "a left-handed twist." The country wasn't prepared for a screwball Billy the Kid. "The film is so strange it disappeared," admits Arthur Penn. But European critics loved *The Left-Handed Gun*. André Bazin of *Cahiers du Cinéma* saw America's dark, hysterical underbelly in Penn's skewered Wild West. It was as if the Kid had some kind of static or ice storm inside his brain.

Such storms were peculiar to left-handers, who lived in an internal planet of extremes. Southpaws "are apt to be extremely dull or extremely bright," overachievers like Einstein, Picasso, Julius Caesar, Alexander the Great, Napoleon Bonaparte, Charlie Chaplin, Leonardo da Vinci, Beethoven, Lewis Carroll, Oprah Winfrey, and Mark Twain . . . or lost men and women, stuck in some asylum, without a language of their own.

But what is the nature of this ice storm in the left-hander's head? We're all *contralateral*, that is, we have a "dueling" brain: the left hemisphere controls the right hand and the right hemisphere controls the left. But the left hemisphere is also the center of language—damage to this side of the brain will usually cause an impairment of speech and an inability to deal with the written or spoken word, so that language suddenly becomes a chaotic jungle. But this jungle is quite complex. "The vast majority of left-handers are as left-brained for language as their right-handed counterparts." And if the "birth trauma" in left-handers causes some kind of neurological shiver in the left hemisphere, then this *shiver* is completely paradoxical and almost impossible to define, except as Coren says, left-handedness is not only the mark of the devil, but a possible sign of neurosis, rebellion, creativity, and criminality.

And if autism is one of the common maladies of the left-hander, then certain games, such as ping-pong and chess, might be a southpaw's way of singing and soothing himself—of finding another, alternative language. It's no accident that an inordinate number of chess champions and architects have been left-handed. Architecture, like chess, can be considered a game where one has to visualize constantly shifting patterns—with their own mathematical music.

But there are pitfalls in *overinterpreting* the powers and imperfections of left-handers. I was convinced that Bobby Fischer had all the typical signs of "the left-hander syndrome." He was almost pathological in his aggression on the chessboard, neurotic, "more anxious about nearly everything," as left-handers often are. His I.Q. wasn't above average, yet he had the maddening ability to recall every move of every game he'd ever played, like some idiot savant . . . or an autistic child who was singing to himself, and all moves on the board, past, present, and future, were like the prisms of some immense melody that he'd memorized. He was a fictional paradox, like one of Borges' characters, Funes the Memorious, who literally dies because of the unbearable burden of his memory. Funes can't forget a single moment of his life. But he has little sense of self. "His own face in the mirror, his own hands, surprised him on every occasion." He's lost in a whirlwind of details and drowns in them—his own left-handed twist. "I have more memories in myself alone than all men have had since the world was a world. . . ." And so I looked for proof of Fischer's left-handedness. I tracked him on the web, and finally found a picture of Bobby moving a pawn . . . with his right hand.

COREN CONDEMNS US TO AN early grave, but he isn't unsympathetic to our woes. Left-handers, he tells us, "may be at risk from an environment that has been specifically set up for the safety and the convenience of right-handers." From can openers to power tools and locks on a door, we're always bumbling around, and no wonder our lives are at risk: 89 percent of us are "more likely to have an accident-related injury requiring medical attention than a right-hander," *and* "six times more likely to die from causes initiated by accident-related injuries." The right-handed world, according to Coren, is "devouring" left-handers . . . just as Lewis Carroll's Wonderland almost devours Alice. She can hardly negotiate in a world that is "curiouser and curiouser," where cats grin like lunatics, rabbits hop around and talk in riddles and rhymes, where Alice is obliged to play croquet with flamingos and hedgehogs as her mallets and balls, where little soldiers twist in opposite directions from Alice, which is always hazardous to her health.

Studies more recent than Coren's haven't supported his elegy for left-handers. But whether Coren is right or wrong, he has at least introduced us to the left-hander syndrome. In sports such as polo, where strict patterns of play have to be observed, and collisions can be fatal for horse *and* rider, southpaws have become an endangered species. Huntington, the premier polo club in England, has forbidden left-handers onto the field. "Even Prince Charles, heir to the throne," and "a natural left-hander, has been forced to play polo right-handed if he wishes to play at all."

Prince Charles is part of a left-handed elite. Queen Victoria, the Queen Mother, Queen Elizabeth II, Charles, and Prince William could have jumped out of Lewis Carroll—lefties taking revenge on a right-handed world. But it's hard to fathom that the Queen Mother, Elizabeth II, and Victoria all suffered from some malediction that endowed them with difficult pregnancies, as Coren hints.

And if lefties are so scarce, why have we had a spate of southpaw Presidents in the second half of the twentieth century? Harry Truman, Gerald Ford, Ronald Reagan, George Bush Sr., and Bill Clinton (though Ronald Reagan was taught to eat and scribble with his right hand). And Gerald Ford is a bumbler like me. "He was always bumping into his honor guard, colliding with members of his entourage," because he couldn't negotiate with the right-handers around him, he couldn't fit into their dance, and he was laughed right out of office. . . .

BUT FORD'S OWN MISHAPS bring us right back to ping-pong, where I've found my particular niche. I'm ranked 11013 among all the registered players in France. How will I ever climb on the backs of the other 11012? I don't have a Chinaman's chance (particularly when the Chinese are the very best players on the planet, wiping out everybody at the 1999 World's). I'm ambitious, like most left-handers, but win or lose, I've learnt how to "talk" at the table. My nickname at the club is "maître," because I scribble books. I take my lickings. And that terrain around the table has become my own little corner of France. . . .

But there was another table, right outside my window, in the square Georges Lamarque. Two tables, in fact, composed of pebbled concrete, with concrete legs, and a concrete net. It required a special fluidity, a special dance, to play on a pebbled surface, with a net that had no suppleness at all. And the square, named after a hero of the Resistance who died on September 8, 1944, was in reality a little park and playground with a sliding pond, two little rocking cars that sat on coiled springs, and a gigantic sandbox. Georges Lamarque had been the captain of a network called the *Druides-Alliance*, and the word *druides* stuck in my head, gave the square a magical persona, as if it were on hallowed ground. I'd often read in the park, sniff the fumes of passing automobiles, until I had tears in my eyes. But there was another reason for my vigilance in the park. It had its own ping-pong champion, a guy in glasses, with a slight limp. He always wore a shirt and tie when he played. I imagined him as a pharmacist, dispensing magic potions like some druid.

He was the neighborhood champ, a ferocious attacker who took on all challengers, spotting them five or ten points, but he wasn't a money player, like the Needle, wasn't a gambler at heart. His own reward was the sheer pleasure of a sure kill. He would balance himself on his game leg and twirl his body around as he attacked, with a terrifying grimace. I wondered if he'd have torso problems, like Philou and Patrick Chila. He always won and his reputation spread to other playgrounds, other arrondissements. He called himself Lord Byron, though unlike Byron, he didn't have a genuine clubfoot. But no *pongiste* could defeat him, or exploit his game leg.

And so, on a hot afternoon, the 11013th ranked player in France took his *picot* out of its sheath and waited on line near the table that was furthest from the sandbox and the little rocking cars, the one that Lord Byron had appropriated for himself. I was only another gadfly to him, an irritant he'd have to swat away with his bat, which looked like some cheap item he'd picked up at a children's store. But it served him well on the bumpy concrete—like a druid's weapon.

He'd mastered each millimeter of pebble. He knew the different hops of his terrain. But he hadn't encountered my own "pebbles," the curious pimples of a picot. Lord Byron wouldn't allow me to warm up. He had other local champions on line. But that was his fatal flaw. He couldn't anticipate the singularity of my music, the unique curl of the ball coming off the pebbles. Suddenly he had no terrain. And the surface that had been so familiar to him wasn't familiar at all.

Was I antisocial in my devilish will to win? I could have kept the game close. But I annihilated Lord Byron, destroyed him at his own table. He couldn't slam or shovel the ball over the concrete net. I beat Byron 21-6. He demanded a rematch. I beat him 21-3, as I got more and more used to his terrain.

He didn't utter a word. He slid the bat under his arm and limped out of the park. I had no desire to take his place, to become the new Lord Byron of the square Lamarque. But he never returned to his table. And perhaps I wasn't as much of a criminal as I thought. I was only a brat. I'd upset the ecology of that little park. Lord Byron belonged there, with the sandbox and the rocking cars.

I'd see him from time to time, pumping on a bicycle, where his limp wasn't apparent. He wouldn't give me the slightest sign of recognition. He looked beyond my own glance. He flew on his bicycle, and I couldn't return to read in the park. I'd banished myself, one more Billy the Kid, a left-handed gun.

NINE

Ping-Pong Diplomacy

LET'S GO BACK A BIT, to 1971. An odd couple ruled the White House. President Nixon, a paranoid anti-Semite, and Henry Kissinger, his German-Jewish-American magus, who'd bump into each other five or six times a day. "The President needs Henry," said one of Kissinger's men. "You've got to realize that the President isn't doing his homework these days. It's only Henry who pulls us through." Nixon was a Red-bater who'd been savaging Chou En-lai and Chairman Mao for twenty years, and Kissinger was a Harvard prof who'd studied Mao's poems and philosophies. But Henry and Richard loved to intrigue in the corridors of the White House and were fond of "eavesdropping . . . backbiting" and "power plays." Both of them were in deep shit. The country was mired in Vietnam. Nixon had lost his popularity and was almost a prisoner in the White House. He couldn't stray from Pennsylvania Avenue without being greeted by war protestors. Yet his old enemies, Chou and Chairman Mao, would soon bail him out. By 1971 China had more to fear from the Soviet Union, which had troops massed at its borders, than from the U.S., whose "mad dogs" were much, much farther away.

Kissinger would make a secret trip to China, called Marco Polo I. And the Chinese found a perfect prelude for rapprochement with the "mad dogs." Ping-pong. It had no diplomatic relations with the U.S. and no American was allowed to enter China, but the American national table tennis team happened to be in Nagoya, Japan, for the 1971 World Championships, where they were rapidly eliminated, when the call came from China.

Graham Steenhoven, formerly the master of Michigan ping-pong and now president of the USTTA, had to check with the White House. He was given clearance within thirty minutes. It would be a goodwill tour, visits to Canton, Peking, and Shanghai, and exhibition matches with the Chinese. "Friendship First, Competition Second" the Chinese would stress. And thus began "The Week that Changed the World."

Tim Boggan, who was covering the championships as editor of *Table Tennis Topics*, said that the Chinese invitation arrived "like a bolt out of the blue." Suddenly all the lowly American ping-pong reporters at Nagoya were besieged with offers to become foreign correspondents. Tim chose the *New York Times*. He was caught in a maelstrom. "Only the death of Kennedy got more play." Half the players were still in their teens. And their images were appearing everywhere.

They flew to Hong Kong, crossed the border into mainland China. Among them were fifteen-year-old Judy Bochenski, dressed in a miniskirt; nineteen-year-old John Tannehill, a sociology major at the University of Cincinnati, who'd cropped his long curly hair for the World's and looked like a strange monk in Farmer Brown overalls; George Brathwaite, a black man from Guyana in his late thirties (he was the one whom cardiologist Steve Horowitz had singled out for his ability to resist the aging process); twenty-year-old Connie Sweeris, a dental assistant from Grand Rapids and the team's top women's player; seventeen-year-old Olga Soltesz; Glenn Cowan, the nineteen-year-old "hippie opportunist in purple passion shirt and tie-dye, leper-like trousers," who wore a great floppy hat over his long dark "D'Artagnan locks" and kept trying to get his face on the cover of *Life* magazine; Errol Resek, former ping-pong champion of the Dominican Republic, who would later do time in Alaska as part of a bumbling band of criminals; team captain Jack Howard; Steenhoven; Tim Boggan; and Dick Miles, who'd come to Japan as a journalist, but would be recognized throughout Shanghai as America's greatest ping-pong champion, though he was utterly *unremembered* in his home town of Manhattan. But in Hong Kong, Miles and his mates were instant celebrities. "Now I know how the president and John Wayne feel," said Olga, who was mobbed wherever she went.

When these curious diplomats rode on the train to Canton, Connie Sweeris said, "I feel like I'm going into a blank." They saw "endless rice paddies . . . and buffaloes knee-deep in water." At Canton they were greeted by the eerie sounds of recorded military music . . . and "a ring of applauding Chinese," Tim Boggan recalls. "Nothing happened on their faces. They were looking at you like zombies."

Tim was startled by the "three-storey pictures of Mao" all over the place, "the lack of paint on the buildings," the unpaved streets. "There was so much dirt . . . it looked like a bombed-out area." And the hotels were terribly plain, as if "nobody had used them for decades."

The "diplomats" had bodyguards and interpreters, but they weren't prevented from wandering about. People would swirl around them. "We could have been from another planet."

Steenhoven, through his interpreter, asked one of the Chinese, "When was the last time you saw an American?"

"On the battlefield," the man said. "During the Korean War."

Steenhoven was "a corporation kind of guy . . . a forty-year Chrysler management man," who tried to do the impossible—stamp "the known and the unknown all in a predictable line." He warned the players "We don't want the peace sign" (a clenched fist). "We don't want you to call them Chinamen . . . . Men, don't reach into your pockets, and women, don't reach into your purses when you're around Premier Chou. Someone might think you're reaching for a gun."

But Steenhoven's diplomats were a band of unruly children. One of them developed shingles, another cried that she couldn't find a McDonald's anywhere and how could she live without a hamburger? Tannehill's "head was fucked up," according to Tim. "He'd have vacant lapses" in his Farmer Browns. "At first John thought he might like to stay in China an extra week or forever—that of course caused a great stir." Steenhoven went ballistic. But he couldn't banish Tannehill from the team. John was just being John.

And Steenhoven? The man from Chrysler was sculpting his own ideal team. He posed "in happy togetherness" with his American boys and girls on top of the Great Wall and was "immortalized" on the cover of *Time* magazine. "I've seen Hadrian's Wall between Scotland and England, but it's just a pebble by comparison."

He was playing Henry Kissinger and Chairman Mao, the diplomat of diplomats *and* a terrible tyrant. "Where I can use my authority as USTTA President, I will to the *nth* degree . . . . I remind you again that I will be sole arbiter of your actions. . . . We are a history-making group."

He would politick behind the team's back, conspire with Washington *and* Peking. He had a single obsession—to reciprocate the "Friendship Match" and have the Chinese team visit America, particularly Detroit, where he could exercise his own little bit of glory. "He had always to be on the lookout—to keep the road to Detroit clear for the Chinese. He had always this secret vigil," Tim writes in *Ping-Pong Oddity*, his memoir of the trip.

But Cowan and Tannehill frustrated him, wouldn't "act as Americans act," which in Steenhoven's vocabulary meant docile and obedient. "I came here as a human being," John Tannehill told Tim. "I'm a person before I'm a table tennis player. Responsibility to Graham means control, domination . . . China knows it can beat us at table tennis. They brought us over here for the political consequences."

Tannehill believed in Mao's Little Red Book. Mao was telling him "to search after truth. To be a philosopher . . . To look behind what is there."

For John, the Great Wall was no big deal, a bunch of stones built "to keep out the Mongols." He'd been running up and down the wall in his Farmer Browns. He saw it as a political act. "Everything I eat, everything I think, everything I do has to be political."

He was becoming a pain in the ass, with his mystical Maoism. "It was as if, without knowing it, he'd gotten himself trapped in an empty building, in one dark closed corridor of thought after another, and after running up and down the stairs . . . he now sat, high up, alone in the dark, in a corner of the one empty room he by chance found open—when suddenly, behold, somebody came in, threw a light switch, and John awoke, overjoyed, to find himself in a lively, crowded classroom."

Cowan was also a pain in the ass, wheeling and dealing whenever he could, hoping to get the "equipment rights" to the Chinese team's bats, tables, and balls. He would answer reporters' questions as if he were Tim. "Because, you know, when things get too complicated or too stupid, I project into a different body." He was thumbing his nose at

Steenhoven and chasing fame by the tail. "We're going to play 50,000 tournaments when we get back," he told Tannehill.

But John got sick in Peking, perhaps with dysentery or the result of dehydration after jogging on the Great Wall. Jack Howard took him to a hospital. "Jesus, don't leave me here! Don't leave me here!" Tannehill screamed in his delirium. And Howard promised that he wouldn't leave China without him.

Tannehill wasn't a prima donna. He was, in Tim's mind, simply naïve. Cowan was the show-off. He would wear red bandannas around his head, put his shoe on the table during a match, parade in his long hair. He'd become the pal of Chuang Tse-tung, three-times World Champion and perhaps the most popular man in his country, *after* Chairman Mao and Chou En-lai. In Nagoya, Glenn had practiced with Chuang and had gotten a ride back to his hotel on the Chinese bus. He arrived at the hotel with a silk-screen portrait of the Hanchow Mountains, a gift from Chuang, which he promptly revealed to whatever photographers were around. And once he was inside China, he gathered photographers around him again as he presented Chuang with a red, white, and blue "peace" shirt. Later, when he returned to the U.S., a celebrity now, part of America's "miracle team," he tossed his floppy hat on stage at an Elton John concert and *Rolling Stone* named him "Groupie of the Year."

Steenhoven would have probably killed him if he could, but he couldn't even stop Glenn from getting high on hashish and offering to get his Chinese interpreter high with him. That was the real beginning of ping-pong diplomacy. . . .

The Chinese were mesmerized by Glenn. He would jump over a barrier to retrieve a ball at his matches in Peking and Shanghai. The audience was composed mainly of Red Guards. "Soldiers that looked like 20th-century robots saw a cavalier—and for a moment they were powerless, were captured: Glenn had caught the romance in their hearts."

TIM REMEMBERS WALKING up the red carpeted stairs of the Great Hall of the People in Peking on his way to meet premier Chou En-lai. There was a gigantic painting of *Mao's Ode to Snow* on the rear wall, with the picture of an endless snow peak. "We came toward it and soon we were *in* the ice and snow world of the painting and beyond was the country of Shangri-La." Tim said to Chou En-lai, through an interpreter, that the *image* of Mao's ode "was like coming into a heaven of poetry."

Tim grasped that the Premier was perfectly fluent in English. But Chou En-lai was a much subtler diplomat than Nixon or Henry Kissinger. He waited a bit to prepare his answer. "Perhaps you overpraise it," he said of Mao's magic mountain.

Tim also chatted with the seventy-three-year-old premier about ping-pong. Chou was a *pongiste.* "Though I'm advanced in age, I can still play—but that's the only sport I am able to do. I play slowly, and to hold the bat is not so strenuous."

Dick Miles and Tim played at an Old Boys' match in Shanghai. "Miles was out of practice." He lost the first game. But like Reisman, he'd also been a money player, and he sang into the stands, "Would anyone like to bet that I win the second one?" He did win. And in the third game, he realized that his Chinese opponent was trying to throw the match. Miles wouldn't allow it. "He says to the umpire, 'Let's call it a draw.' The umpire's face goes incomprehensible. He's wounded, upset. The game has to go on. And now it's Miles who throws the match . . . he had this stubborn pride." He wouldn't fall into the choreography of a choreographed match.

But the team matches were choreographed in much the same way. The Chinese marveled at a black man—Brathwaite—on the American team. He was cheered when he played, and the Chinese let him win. "It seemed like we put up a good fight, but in reality we couldn't have won a match . . . the people who came to the matches were conscripted soldiers or policeman. A light would flash above their heads whenever they weren't clapping enough."

The Chinese players almost seemed embarrassed about winning. "They were anxious to learn from us." But the Americans had precious little to teach. The Chinese had just come out of their own crazy Cultural Revolution, where Mao had withdrawn his ping-pongers from international tournaments. But they were still the best players on the planet, in a league of their own. And the Americans, who'd once ranked second, right behind the Hungarians, were now a threat to no one. But Chou En-lai had just given them a soft parachute, where they could land in safety. He'd allowed the "paper tigers" to look like warriors in front of the whole world. And he was the real choreographer, not Henry Kissinger. "Regard a Ping-Pong ball as the head of your capitalist enemy," Mao had once written. "Hit it with your socialist bat and you have won a point for the fatherland." It was Mao who'd mythologized the ping-pong table, had millions of them delivered to schools and meeting halls, as "a people's exercise," writes Stefan Kanfer in "The Demonic Game of Plock-Plack" (The *New York Times Magazine,* April 2, 1972). But now "plock-plank" was replacing the boom-boom of cannons and bombs. There were fierce opponents in both countries to any kind of thaw, but Chou En-lai had quieted the white *and* red devils, made them purr with the help of a ping-pong ball.

"Day after day in China you couldn't start out with anything predictable, anything to hold on to," Tim wrote. What struck him most was "the alien nature of the place . . . all those people on bicycles, the dust, the constant honking of horns," and the mystery he felt beside the Great Wall, when a band of ping-pong players and their mentors were the only tourists. "The snake-like stone" continued to haunt Tim, "to lie there in my imagination," even the broken remnants that would soon be repaired and turn the Great Wall into China's number-one tourist attraction. He preferred to see the wall as an enduring wonder of art, not the "repair work of unendurable man."

And what about Glenn Cowan, America's D'Artagnan? "I loved China," he said. "I loved the Chinese. Where else, man, would you see a child of three carrying a child of two in his arms?"

After their eight days in China, the ping-pong diplomats flew back to the U.S. with a great deal of hurly-burly and hullabaloo. "Now that I've gone to China, gee, I've become famous," Cowan said underneath his floppy hat. "I think I could negotiate between Chou En-lai and Nixon quite easily."

Miles had already appeared on *Wide World of Sports*, and Tim and some of the team members would appear on the Johnny Carson and Dick Cavett shows, and would be invited to France in the summer of '71 by *Paris Match*. They were the new American heroes—"les Pongistes U.S."—practitioners of a much maligned, almost forgotten sport. *Ping-pong*, which most Americans likened to tiddlywinks and other children's games . . . until the China trip.

Tannehill would drop out of college and continue his mystical Maoism. Judy Bochenski would write an article for *Seventeen* and reign as grand marshall of the Portland Rose Festival Parade. Tim would return to *Table Tennis Topics* and his job as professor of Romantic poetry at Long Island University. Miles went back to his Stiga Robot, which could compete with his own deadly chop. "I

have a machine, a girl friend and a dog. Those, and the game, are all I need."

THINGS QUIETED DOWN FOR THE "diplomats." And then on February 17, 1972, Nixon flew to Peking on Air Force One with his magus. John Wayne had warned him about "that Jew, Kissinger" and had written to the White House, declaring that the China trip was "a real shocker." But Nixon had already told *Time* magazine: "If there is anything I want to do before I die, it is to go to China."

On his arrival in Peking, Nixon had a Secret Service man block the aisle of Air Force One, so that he could exit alone, without his magus. Chou En-lai was also alone, standing on the tarmac without a hat.

After lunch, Kissinger and Nixon had an unexpected audience with Chairman Mao, that frail old demigod who could barely stand. Nixon told Mao that his writings had "changed the world."

"I haven't been able to change it," the chairman said. "I've only been able to change a few places in the vicinity of Peking."

Thus went the ping-pong match between President Nixon and Chairman Mao. . . .

Of course, Nixon's trip had helped Steenhoven with his own mission—to keep the road open to Detroit. The Chinese were coming! A ping-pong delegation sixteen-strong had accepted the USTTA's invitation to visit the U.S. and tour with the American team. It was Easter 1972, exactly a year after Steenhoven's boys and girls had gone right through the looking glass, into a country that had been closed by the Cultural Revolution. But this time Steenhoven wouldn't tolerate any embarrassments. He handpicked America's ten players, and the list didn't include Tannehill or Reisman and Miles, "the bad boys of American ping-pong," whom Steenhoven had already suspended once. Tannehill sulked, Reisman hollered murder, and Miles shrugged. "At first I thought this should be a big coup for table tennis, that we should make a tremendous big splash, but he" (Steenhoven) "didn't agree. 'This is bigger than table tennis, far bigger than any individual,' he said, and I think he's correct."

Finally, after a prod from Miles himself and many other players, Steenhoven relented, and Tannehill was put on the team. But Steenhoven wouldn't use him or Cowan in a match. The man from Chrysler was getting even. "Both of them had left a bonfire of dirty underwear at the team's hotel in Peking," Tim Boggan recalls, and the poor Chinese had to sneak that "bonfire" back onto the American bus.

The Chinese weren't innocents abroad, like the Americans had been. Goodwill ambassadors who didn't leave their dirty underwear behind, they were programmed to win . . . and also dump certain matches. Chou En-lai had probably choreographed most of their moves. Nixon greeted them at the White House.

Tim Boggan, who was there with the American team, noticed that "Nixon wanted to make this as quick as possible." The ceremony was in the Rose Garden. "Nixon strides right past the American team. 'Don't you want to meet the players who went to China?' Olga Soltesz asks. 'Oh, yes,' Nixon says. 'I didn't know you were here.'"

That, it seems to me, punctures the entire myth of ping-pong diplomacy. The American players meant nothing at all to Dick. He was utterly self-absorbed, a man sealed inside the narrower and narrower reach of the Oval Office.

And what about that *other* president, Graham Steenhoven, who believed that the Friendship Matches were "bigger than table tennis," that by winnowing out the American team, laundering it "of the socially suspicious," he could impose himself

upon American history? But as Murray Kempton warned in *Esquire*: "History is a series of mistakes made by persons who think they are the cause when they are only the coincidence."

Steenhoven wasn't able to *seize the day*, as Chairman Mao had advised in one of his poems ("Reply to Comrade Kuo Mo-Jo").

The west wind scatters leaves over Changan,
And the arrows are flying, twanging.
So many deeds cry out to be done . . .
Ten thousand years are too long.
Seize the day, seize the hour!

The man from Chrysler wanted to control *chaos*, but he couldn't. That chaos included Reverend Carl McIntyre of the radical religious right, whose followers taunted the Chinese and chanted that Mao had murdered millions upon millions of Christian souls.

At Cobo Hall, in Detroit, where the Chinese played their first match, "a dead rat was floated out of the balcony via a small parachute and landed at the feet" of a Chinese player. The rat wore a red coat with the name *Kissinger* on it.

Police dogs sniffed for nitroglycerin at the hotel where the Chinese and the American teams stayed. McIntyre and his men hounded the Chinese wherever they went, whether it was Disneyland, DC, or the UN. There were also antiwar protestors afoot. "Send us our POWs, not ping-pong players," they said.

But Steenhoven played the blind man, oblivious to most of what was around him. During lunch at a Chrysler assembly plant, he took a paddle out of his briefcase and challenged former World Champion Chuang Tse-tung to a five-point match. Chuang toyed with Steenhoven, letting him score a couple of points.

And Steenhoven continued to live in Humpty Dumpty land, trying to turn the American team into mechanical soldiers. He dressed the men in blue blazers, the women in orange turtlenecks and white pantsuits, had them rehearse before every match, so they could march in step, as if they were members of some magical chorus line, instead of idiosyncratic ping-pongers who couldn't earn a living from the game, while the Chinese could practice forever, since they were supported by the state.

Chuang would perform card tricks as the teams hopped from place to place; he'd pluck cards from behind his back, "like Houdini handcuffing himself." In Memphis, where the two teams met at the Mid-South Coliseum, the stands were empty. There were only *three* registered ping-pong players in the whole town. And Tim Boggan couldn't understand why Memphis had been chosen, until he realized that Steenhoven was up to his old corporate tricks. This particular Friendship Match had been funded by Holiday Inn, whose chairman of the board had welcomed the Chinese to Tennessee . . . and the two teams dined and slept in one of the chairman's inns.

The Americans and the Chinese might have filled Madison Square Garden, but they never played in Manhattan. Steenhoven must have felt that New York would be too much of a circus, that there was a risk of mayhem. And so they had their match out on Long Island, at the Nassau Coliseum, in the middle of a rainy afternoon, while vendors sold Paddle Power Love Necklaces with emblems of crossed ping-pong bats and miniature Chinese and American flags.

Paddle Power: the totem words of the Friendship Matches, American-style. One form of hucksterism after another. It was Tannehill, the young sociology student, who had predicted a year earlier that the matches in America would become a farce, captive to Chrysler and General Motors . . . and Holiday Inn. But Tannehill wasn't with the team. He'd cursed Steenhoven after the man from Chrysler wouldn't let him play in Detroit and ran back to Ohio.

The Americans and the Chinese flew out to Hollywood, visited the Universal lot, where they saw Vincent Price and Edgar Bergen waiting on line outside the commissary. Who remembers Bergen now? He was a ventriloquist, famous in the forties, who appeared on the radio and the big screen with a wisecracking puppet: Charlie McCarthy, who wore a monocle and was nothing but a naughty brat. It's curious, but Steenhoven, in every photograph I saw of him, bears an uncanny resemblance to Bergen. He's Bergen's double. And if Charlie McCarthy ever clutched a ping-pong paddle, he could have replaced America's entire team, as Graham's naughty child. . . .

Friendship II couldn't possibly have had the aura and the eclat of Friendship I, when a bunch of scratchy Americans, losers fresh from Japan—a girl in a miniskirt, with her French fries, a guy in a floppy hat—managed, in all their naiveté and unspectacular talent, to help half the world peek at China.

How could Chuang Tse-tung, with all his card tricks, top that? He was the hit of the tour, and not because of his championships. He lent the Chinese a friendly, familiar face. He was an official spokesman, the deputy from Peking to the People's National Congress—it was, according to Tim, like having Babe Ruth or Hank Aaron as your own congressman. That was real paddle power! But he also had a warmth and a grace that charmed the Americans and a razzle-dazzle that could confuse them. "It's dangerous to be a winner," he said. "You can be deceived. Though ping-pong is a highly competitive sport, there is no real victory or defeat. There is always both."

And with that conundrum, Chuang and his teammates boarded the Chinese jet clipper, *Glory of the Skies* (actually a Pan Am 707), on their way to Latin America and yet another Friendship Match.

TEN

The Manchurian Candidate

PUSH FORWARD TWENTY-FIVE YEARS. It's July 24, 1997. We're at the United Nations Delegates' Lounge in New York. Behind us is a huge tapestry of the Great Wall, a gift from the People's Republic. We're celebrating the twenty-fifth anniversary (or twenty-sixth, depending on your own calendar and calculation) of Ping-Pong Diplomacy. There are two hundred fifty guests. A table has been set up in the cavernous lounge, and China's current stars, Women's World Champion Deng Yaping and Men's Olympic Champion Lui Guoliang, demonstrate their skills, attacking the ball with warp-speed precision that dazzles the eye and forces us to blink. It's almost half a century away from the mythic Miles-Reisman matches at Lawrence's, where a single point might last eight minutes, and the duel between the Needle's Atomic Blast and Miles' dancing feet and relentless windmill chop felt like an instant of eternity. . . .

Both Miles and Reisman are among the celebrants at the U.N. So are Connie Sweeris, Judy Hoarfrost, née Bochenski, no longer wearing miniskirts, George Brathwaite, who'd worked at the U.N. and was instrumental in arranging this exhibition match . . . and Chang Shih-lin, captain of China's '72 Friendship Team, a little heavier now. During the Memphis stop in '72, Chang had talked to Miles about his young boy, whom he was training to become a champion.

"What's his secret?" Miles had asked.

"He plays with a little paddle."

"How does he do?"

"He breaks all the lightbulbs in the building."

Henry Kissinger, Nixon's former magus, is also at the reunion. "Only once in a while something happens in diplomacy which transcends the drafting of cables and the formal messages that are sent," Kissinger tells the celebrants. "And by adding a human dimension to what seemed to be a very frozen situation, the table tennis team"—Connie Sweeris & Co.—"really made a tremendous contribution."

Who wants to argue with Henry Kissinger? Who could possibly win? But I suspect that the innocents abroad were little more than ciphers in a power struggle that swirled far above their heads. It would take all the clatter of game theory, with its emphasis on conflict, strategy, and chance, to deal with the wiles and the "warfare" of ping-pong diplomacy. There were rumors running around that Nixon "dabbled in the sport," that he'd been practicing for months at his Camp David retreat, preparing for Friendship II. But I doubt that he'd ever held a paddle in his hand during his presidency. It was one more bit of disinformation from Nixon's entourage. He'd used the Chinese, as the Chinese were using him, in the ultimate ping-pong match of "survival." Washington and Peking were playing blind man's bluff, where both winners and losers were caught in a labyrinth. At least the Chinese *pongistes* were a conscious part of Peking's strategy: they didn't have to be *told* to win. They could have done that in their dreams. But they had to make the Americans look a bit better than they were or ping-pong diplomacy wouldn't have worked. How could the Chinese talk friendship while they massacred the Americans? It wasn't a simple task to prop up a team that was so unpredictable.

The Americans were manipulated by everyone: the Chinese players, Peking, and their own government, which couldn't have cared less about their individual fate, as Nixon made clear when he practically snubbed them in the Rose Garden. But the man from Chrysler would see none of this. "We're table tennis players," he told one reporter after certain politicians had complained about the "propaganda advantage" the Chinese had plucked from Friendship I and the American team's presence in Peking. According to Graham, purists like him *and* his boys and girls couldn't be stranded in the middle of a propaganda war.

A week after Friendship I, Steenhoven flew without the "miracle team" to meet with Nixon in D.C.

"Hello, Graham," said the president, while photographers surrounded them like jackals.

And because Nixon had really nothing to say while their picture was being taken, he whispered to Steenhoven, "Let's talk about anything. How much is a ping-pong ball?"

"A quarter," Steenhoven said, and that was his contribution to this tête-á-tête.

But he hadn't come to the twenty-fifth-year reunion. He was in his mid-eighties by then, yet it wasn't like Steenhoven to give up center stage and withdraw from the world. Was he sick perhaps and already disenchanted with ping-pong? Nobody knows. And what about Graham's nemesis, John Tannehill? He also hadn't come. He'd abandoned the sport, hadn't played in fifteen years. But there was something significant about the absence of these two men. Of all the Americans, they were the two most evident *players* in Nixon's and Chou's ping-pong battle.

For Steenhoven, Tannehill was like a creature out of *The Manchurian Candidate*, who'd been brainwashed by the Chinese, like Sergeant Raymond Shaw (Lawrence Harvey), in John

Frankenheimer's film, who could explode any minute and wreck Graham's chances of finalizing Friendship II. Steenhoven was "sitting on a time bomb," and that bomb was Tannehill himself, whom the American and Canadian press had pilloried, just because Tannehill wanted to stay in China an extra week. He was branded a Communist tool, and people began to wonder if Graham had become his own "Manchurian Candidate," brainwashed by the Red Chinese. Tannehill did pin a Mao button to his Farmer Browns, did cut his hair like a Buddhist monk, but he wasn't trying to bedevil Steenhoven. He was, according to Glenn Cowan and Tim, "like a camera on wheels rolling madly about without any kind of directing intelligence, any personal I," a persona in search of itself. "It was psychic sickness that bugged him." Unlike Cowan, who was constantly performing, playing to the crowd, hoping to merchandise the Chinese team's equipment and become a table tennis tycoon, "John had run wild because he had no function at all . . . John was footloose."

And Steenhoven couldn't rein him in. He was a curious, contradictory soul, this man from Chrysler. Like Reisman and Miles, whom he seemed to detest, he'd had his own wild side. He'd been a marble hustler as a child, a sharp who'd swindled pennies from kids on his block. But he'd stamped that out of his curriculum vitae. "I have nothing to sell but my integrity," he said. Bespectacled, white-haired, a partisan of Chrysler and ping-pong for over forty years, he wanted to push back the dark. "If we don't adhere to standards, we have utter chaos."

Tim recognized all of the contradictions. Graham was the magic gardener. If he could nourish the seeds of Friendship I and II, "no nightmare . . . would ever be possible." But there was still the wicked child in him, who realized that Tannehill and the others would do whatever they wanted to do, "even if it cracked the crazy looking-glass of our togetherness."

At times he was an impossible tyrant. "I began to think that if he were to come on like Captain Queeg," the paranoid, impossible ship commander in *The Caine Mutiny*, "we could relieve him of his command." But, of course, this particular Queeg happened to triumph. "He talked to the Chinese the way they wanted, or expected, him to talk—in a way I never could . . . He managed, with or without us, the job of his life."

And he became the hero of his time. After Friendship II, he would receive the Detroit-Windsor International Freedom Award, previously given to JFK and Martin Luther King, and the March of Dimes Citizen Award. But awards were never enough. He was stuck inside the obscurity of the game itself. During Friendship II, while he toured with Chuang Tse-tung, he would lament to Tim, "I've fought for table tennis every step of the way. And they don't know me. They don't know Steenhoven. Chuang takes my hand when I'm introduced. He introduces me."

Steenhoven was like a little boy again, searching for the piece of candy he could never collect. But John Tannehill fell into a deeper obscurity, in Columbus, Ohio, where he works as an attendant at the American Veterans' donation center (similar to a Salvation Army thrift shop). I felt that Tim had been unfair to John, who may have been footloose in China, but at least was looking for some kind of definition. In 1971 he was the second-best player in the U.S., a sponger who hated sponge and all the technology that surrounded it. "The deadening anti-topspin bat, the oscillating Stiga Robot were ruining the sport . . . anybody could pick up the newest sponge racket and, without any strokes, without any 'touch,' without any anguish from trial and error, could soon be pretty successful . . . until new and improved weapons came his way. In the end, playing the game made you senseless, made you lose all self-expression, made you into a machine."

And the anxiety attacks he suffered in China, the moments of grandeur and *craziness*, were built into the fabric of the trip—the vast unknown of the country itself and the ambiguity of being there as pawns *and* ping-pong players. This cultural and political schizophrenia was shared by everyone, including Graham himself. Tim captured it to perfection in the raw material of *Ping-Pong Oddity*, which is like a marvelous untouched photograph.

Whatever function Tim had—philosopher, foreign correspondent, USTTA official—he was still overwhelmed by China. "I was lost. . . . And though with my limited vantage point I was in a group trying always to look and listen carefully, I was always alone, and sometimes near paralysis."

The Americans were like a bunch of left- handers lost in a right-handed world where everything was upside down. Before the China trip, Miles had gone to the American embassy in Tokyo and met with the in-house "professional China-watcher," begging to be briefed. "There must be a hundred sacred Chinese customs I could violate, just by accident."

The China-watcher rocked in his chair. "Don't steal any dinosaur eggs."

That's how Dick Miles was briefed.

The Americans had to bump around in the heart of darkness and avoid as many dinosaur eggs as they could.

TANNEHILL WAS THE ONE WHO haunted me the most. Like Alice, I grew curiouser and curiouser about him. I called him in Columbus. It was July 2000. And I couldn't imagine Tannehill as a man approaching fifty. He *sounded* like a boy of nineteen, with a very sweet voice.

I asked him how he felt when he was told that the American team was going to China.

"Scared," he said.

"Scared of what?"

"That the Chinese would be doing mysterious things . . . it was dangerous."

He recalled the eerie "Mao music" coming from loudspeakers at the border, "as we were hitting China." The first sight he had of "a bunch of workers working their heads off."

He never saw a single fly in the country. There was a myth surrounding this odd absence. "One day Mao got sick of flies. He told everybody in China to kill one fly. . . ."

And as a player in China, Tannehill "felt totally outclassed. They were throwing games to me," and there was little he could do about it. But he didn't feel boxed in. There was no Big Brother who prevented him from running around Peking and Shanghai. He would walk the streets with Cowan at four a.m., or in the middle of the afternoon, when he noticed "little children making little stone tables and stone nets."

I asked him about Friendship II. "I was a danger to that impression the Americans wanted to make . . . . Steenhoven was calling the shots. He didn't play Cowan or me."

John wasn't able to have one personal chat with the Chinese team. "There was no way to talk to the Chinese outside the interpreters. You couldn't ask a real question." And it bothered Tannehill, both the politics *and* the new technology. He would abandon ping-pong. "Sponge technology was killing the game. There's no dialogue between players, just power shots." He'd started playing again, but with a hard rubber bat.

He didn't like to dwell on Steenhoven or the Chinese trip. "I felt a little bit used by the national spirit of America." The Americans had climbed on his back when he wanted to prolong his stay in China. Everything had become "curiously politicized."

But he did have one powerful reminder of the Friendship Matches. "The Chinese were impressed by our visit." Several people in Columbus had come up to him, refugees from China. One man, who'd been a boy of ten at the time, "remembered everything about the trip. He'd saved a clipping for twenty-eight years, a picture of us on the Great Wall. He'd almost starved during the Cultural Revolution," but he still had that clipping. . . .

IT WAS STILL HARD FOR me to understand how all the hurly-burly over ping-pong during and after Friendship I and II hadn't started a fashion . . . and a craze. It couldn't have been Steenhoven's fault.

"Why didn't ping-pong take off?" I asked Tim Boggan.

"We just didn't have any good players. We were twenty-eighth in the world . . . there was no Bobby Fischer!"

No Bobby Fischer.

Fischer would create a furor when he defeated Boris Spaasky *and* the Soviet Union's stranglehold on chess at Reykjavik, Iceland, and became the new world champion on August 31, 1972, the same year as the second Friendship Match. Ironically, Fischer won all his decisive games in a closed ping-pong room at Laugardscholl, Reykjavik's chess arena. Despite his sullen behavior, Fischer was now an international hero. He'd grown into a peculiar bird. He would wake at four p.m., have breakfast and a pregame snack of sour milk, cheese, herring, black bread, apple and orange juice, and a beverage of barley and malt, half of which he would bring with him to Laugardscholl and devour during the match. His manner ruffled Spaasky and the entire Russian bench. Fischer fought with everyone—the U.S.,

Icelandic, Soviet, and world chess federations, the U.S. Naval Air Station at Keflavik, and the owner of the alley where he loved to bowl, but his picture still appeared on the cover of magazines throughout the world: Bobby wearing a blanket like an Eskimo, Bobby in the presidential suite at the Hotel Loftleidir, Bobby in his split-level retreat outside Reykjavik, Bobby taking a swim . . .

If the Americans had had one genius in Peking, a wizard who could have bitten back at the Chinese, then ping-pong might have prospered. Fischer could bask in isolation, replay the games of all the grandmasters, dead or alive (he never traveled anywhere without his chess books), but ping-pong can't come out of a book. Fischer thrived on loneliness, killing off people at the chessboard, while the Americans were locked within the confines of their own continent, without a single sponsor. "Who in the country was going to watch or remember a ping-pong player?" Tim lamented in his book. "Every top U.S. player's toughest opponent, the one who every time would hit him and drop him to death, was Anonymity."

The Chinese were also locked within their own continent, particularly during the Cultural Revolution, but ping-pong was the national pastime in China, the national sport. You could find tables everywhere, including the railroad station at Peking, which had four hundred ping-pong tables. "The trains never ran on time, and there were always lots of people waiting." Perhaps the four hundred tables are apocryphal. But so what? They still exemplify the Chinese attitude toward ping-pong.

None of the American players at the 1971 World's had been subsidized. Judy Bochenski's classmates at William R. Boone High in Eugene, Oregon, had helped her raise the airfare to Japan from collection jars "placed in the cafeteria and other spots around the school." High school kids had to fill the empty coffers of the USTTA. That was the state of American ping-pong in 1971.

"To be a player you need to practice twelve hours a day and forget about going to school and making money," said Alex Ehrlich, the Chiseler King, who might have been describing the conditions at Lawrence's, when two notorious high school dropouts, Dick Miles and the Needle, gambled and played, gambled and played. But there wasn't a single venue like Lawrence's in 1971. The Americans either worked for a living or went to school . . . with the exception of housewife Connie Sweeris.

China had six million registered players in 1971; the U.S. barely had five thousand. And Chinese coaches started selecting kids very, very early, at six or seven, took them away from their parents by the time they were thirteen, and put them in special schools, where they would practice seven days a week. World Champions Lui Guoliang and Kong Linhgui are best friends who have lived and trained together since they were eleven.

According to Tim, these training schools are very authoritarian. "The players do what the coaches tell them to do," they eat and sleep with a ping-pong bat. Lui Guoliang has little memory outside the sport. He's "always been in table tennis." Like any hypermodern player with a penholder grip, he can use both sides of the racquet by twirling his wrist, destroy an opponent with his forehand and backhand skill.

But I was packed with all the usual myths that "Round Eyes" had about the Chinese and their magical penholder play. "If you're powerful and tall," a particular coach told Tim on his return trip to China in 1979, "you're encouraged to be a shakehands player" (who gripped the handle with a four-finger lock in the traditional European and American manner). "If you've got a naturally flexible wrist and aren't too tall maybe you'll be a penholder."

Tim marveled at the Chinese. "They're so innovative . . . they work hours and hours each day on technique. They're like monks. With that technique they can play competitively into their forties."

In 1979 Tim also visited the table tennis factory at Tientsin. "Every Chinese player must make his pilgrimage there to handpick his own special racket." I was instantly jealous, wishing I could make my own pilgrimage. . . .

Tim was told a story about Hungarian coach Zoltan Berczik, who years ago, when he was European champion, had come to China to train. "But when the first tier Chinese National Team had all beaten him he had to go to the second and then the third. And when they all beat him, he had to go, one by one, to the best teams in Peking . . . and to the local high schools. It was then, finally, when he'd lost to all those players, that he decided to become a coach."

ALL RIGHT, THE CHINESE WERE Zen-like masters of the game, who fixed their mark on ping-pong like a merciless, wounding arrow. But what about the Americans? Weren't there at least seven thousand registered players at the moment, up from five in 1971? Hadn't ping-pong become an Olympic sport in 1988, together with lawn tennis? And wasn't hard cash coming in from the United States Olympic Committee to help the USTTA, now known as USA Table Tennis or USATT, promote the sport and improve its image? And what about those seven thousand registered players? I asked Tim, who glanced at me from behind his glasses.

"Seven thousand? Those figures are always inflated. The seven thousand players aren't constant. There's a turnover every two or three years. A third of the players go away. There are no rewards, no money in table tennis."

It was Tim who succeeded Steenhoven as president of the USTTA. His life had been peaceful as a

professor. "I didn't have enemies . . . all my politics went into table tennis." He tried to change ping-pong's very narrow field. "I began to get good players from all over the world to come to the U.S. Opens. I spent money to invite them and I got hell for it." But long after Tim's own tenure as president, Jean-Philippe Gatien did come to America (Philou won the U.S. Open in 1988).

Tim was still pessimistic. "We need human, not technological, changes. We need exciting fan participation. You go to our Open, and nobody gives a shit who wins."

At the 2000 Open in Fort Lauderdale, Florida, the Needle, touching seventy, lost in an early round. "The less I win, the more famous I become," Marty quipped to his rivals. And it was a prophetic remark. His matches always drew a crowd. He had history on his side, almost sixty years of competition.

Grandmasters, including Lui Guoliang, Sweden's Jan Ove Waldner, and Vladimir Samsonov of Belorusse, ranked number one in the world, were all on a professional tour that stopped in Fort Lauderdale and was supposed to have been the killer event of the Open. But the stands at the Fort Lauderdale Convention Center were utterly deserted except for other players, who'd come to see Samsonov & Co. and could appreciate their devilish spins. World-class ping-pong meant nothing to Floridians.

As Murray Kempton noted thirty years ago, "The new game, all attack, is played with strokes like pistons and spins so unreadable that its masters can make any victim look bad without ever quite able to show the watcher why they themselves are so good."

I still insist that one splendid player in '71 and '72, one improbable genius, might have reshaped our attitude, created a permanent ping-pong fever. But, after all, we did have one such player, even if he happens to be fictional. Robert Zemeckis' film, *Forrest Gump* (1994), tells the story of an idiot savant who learns the game while he's at a rehab center in Saigon (he was shot in the ass). "The secret to this game," says a wounded black vet, "is that no matter what happens, never ever take your eye off the ball." And Forrest never does. He can play with either hand, which means he's a lefty at heart. Soon as he recovers, he's assigned to Special Services and gives exhibitions all over the world. The army also places him on the "All-America Ping-Pong Team" and Gump goes to Peking in '71. He's among "the first Americans to visit the land of China in like a million years, something like that. . . . Somebody said world peace was in our hands."

He plays against a Chinese penholder at Capital Stadium, an enormous image of Mao on the rear wall. Gump stands far from the table. And on the big screen, with the camera's eye at a tilt, ping-pong takes on its own mercurial life, as if the table were the deck of an aircraft carrier, and Gump was slapping balls across some strange infinity.

"When I got home," he says, "I was a national celebrity, famouser even than Captain Kangeroo."

He appears on the *Dick Cavett Show* with John Lennon. He's invited with other members of the team to Nixon's White House. He shakes Nixon's hand and tells him where he's staying.

"I know of a much nicer hotel," Nixon says. "It's brand new, very modern. I'll have my people take care of it for you."

And Nixon steers Gump right to Watergate. Gump catches sight of the Watergate burglars from his window. He calls hotel security. "Their flashlights are keeping me awake."

It's Forrest Gump, ping-pong magician and numbskull, who initiates Nixon's fall.

He also receives a quick twenty-five grand for endorsing a Gump-Mao ping-pong racquet. He's the ultimate innocent, with a 75 IQ, floating somewhere between cretinism and normality. He's also a Medal of Honor winner, like Raymond Shaw, the brainwashed sleeper assassin, who's run by his own mother (Angela Lansbury in a chilling performance as a Russian-Chinese spy). Both Raymond and Forrest Gump are sleepwalkers, but Raymond doesn't have ping-pong to console him.

And Gump's glory is also the game's. It recaptures the period when ping-pong entered the nation's psyche and was part of our folklore. Ping-pong Diplomacy, with all its historic players: Mao, Chou En-lai, Nixon and his magus, the Red Guards sitting at a stadium in Peking, Dick Miles and Tim Boggan, Judy Bochenski, Chuang Tse-tung, Tannehill, Cowan, and the man from Chrysler, who in his monomaniacal way was probably the best tactician that ping-pong has ever known, even if he couldn't make it flower into a sport that Americans would finally embrace.

ELEVEN

Player of the Century

BOGGAN, THE GUY WHO HAS all of ping-pong history inside his head, prepared a list of American ping-pong greats for the new millennium, announcing the Player of the Century, male and female. That was dangerous stuff, more difficult than any time bomb that Steenhoven ever sat on. Tim named Miles as the ultimate men's champion, and Ruth Aarons and Leah "Ping" Neuberger tied as the women's champ. The selection of Aarons was obvious. She was the only American who'd ever won a singles championship in world competition. But "Ping" had a much longer career. Ruth Aarons retired before she was twenty, and "Ping" battled all her life. She won the U.S. Open nine times and the World Mixed Doubles Championship with teenager Erwin Klein. She also sneaked into China in '71 as part of a Canadian delegation . . . moments before the Americans arrived. She was the most active tournament player America has ever had. She *breathed* ping-pong as much as any Chinese champion.

"Mrs. Neuberger's paddle is her passport," the *New York Times* wrote about Leah.

But the men's selection caused much more of a storm. What about Sol Schiff, the first great American champion, a lefty who inspired Dick Miles, whose fingerspin serve drove other players to distraction? Or Lou Pagliaro, who won the U.S. Open four times? Or the Needle himself, who had the highest world ranking of any American male, was much more charismatic than Miles, and was still drawing crowds into the twenty-first century? But the Needle could never "put the lock" on Miles, who managed to win more of their marathon matches. No one could dance like Dick Miles. . . .

George Weinberg, author and psychoanalyst, who actually lived with Marty when he was a boy (Marty's dad took him in when he had nowhere else to stay), remembers the Friday night Reisman-Miles marathons at Lawrence's. "Marty might have been the best player who ever lived if he'd trained . . . people would practically die to see him play Miles." The matches were usually held between one and three in the morning.

George had to rush downtown in the middle of a date with some Bronx beauty in order to get to the match on time. "Everybody came to watch the grandmasters do something they couldn't do." Playing against them, no matter how good you were, "was like telling Shakespeare that you've improved your vocabulary."

Miles "was the heaviest chopper in the country." He could "quadruple his weight" with the "muscle" behind his chop. "The points were long and incredibly dramatic. Miles was never off balance. . . . Miles had an edge. He had better focus. He was greedy, stingy. A guy with that attitude isn't going to lose a point by accident. It was Marty's generosity vs. Miles' stinginess. Stinginess wins. Miles would grant you nothing. It was like a meter ticking in his preconscious. *Always give a little less.* Almost nobody liked Miles, but it helped him to be a champion. . . . Humanness is a flaw in champion play."

And that's how George Weinberg described Dick Miles, the narrowed man. But Tim read Miles in a different fashion, saw him as a very private person, who could wound easily, and had a fierce, almost ungovernable, pride, a loner who didn't have or want Marty's gregariousness, Marty's willingness to share. . . .

He certainly hadn't shared very much with me. But perhaps I was at fault, hadn't considered his intense privacy. Still, I offered to share something with him, my ability to read a manuscript. I knew he'd been working on a novel. "Dick," I said, "I'm a pro." I'd labored with students on their writing for thirty years. I was like a fixer, a mechanic of prose. I offered to have a look at his novel. He was reluctant at first. "I need an agent," he said. "Not another reader."

Was I preparing him for my own kill shot?

"I have an agent," I said. "But I can't recommend your book until I read it. But that's totally up to you."

He sent me the manuscript, *Loving's Folly*, about a melancholic backgammon player who was drummed out of the army and lived with his dog in his mother's old apartment on Manhattan's Upper West Side. The book seemed schizophrenic to me. When Eugene Loving described the world around him, the novel assumed a poetry that recaptured, with muscular *and* lyrical detail, a particular time and a particular place. But when Loving described himself and his "miraculous tool," the book meandered, lost its precision and its charm.

I told that to Miles, spent an hour with him on the phone, crossing out entire passages and checking off descriptions that moved me—a woman's hair, the flight of a hand.

I bullied him a little. "Dick," I said, "you can 'read' every inch of the table, and if I trained a million years, I wouldn't catch a tenth of what you see. Well, prose is my ping-pong table. . . ."

I was ashamed of my own arrogance, but the Player of the Century was touched that I'd spent the time to mark up his manuscript. He invited me to share his Stiga Robot, to hit with him up at his digs on Riverside Drive.

So I went uptown to Dick Miles with my picot. His apartment house gave me a chill: it looked like the building on Riverside Drive where Raymond Shaw had lived *in The Manchurian Candidate*. An incorrigible movie addict, I half expected to see Raymond's karate-chopping valet. But it was Miles who met me at the door. And I could appreciate why he'd been so reticent at first: he didn't look like Bogart anymore. The swagger was gone. He'd slowed down at seventy-five. He'd had a bad fall while visiting London ten or fifteen years ago, and he had a constant ringing in his ears that had almost maddened him for a while.

He couldn't take much pleasure from ping-pong. He hadn't lost his love of the game, but he no longer liked to play, except against his Stiga Robot. He'd bought it in 1968, and the Stiga had never failed him.

Dick's smile wasn't stingy at all. "Wagner said that tempo is everything . . . technique is everything, says Dick Miles."

He approached the Robot, which was attached to the far side of a ping-pong table like an infernal machine, with a curious "bridal veil" that covered up a motor with a pipe that could spit out a ball that no ping-pong player had ever dreamed of. The pipe's little eyehole was like the fierce eye of God. I couldn't "touch" the Robot, read any of its spins. It was Stiga twenty-one, and Jerome zero. "That's not much spin for the Robot," Miles said, "but no human spins that much."

Miles picked up his sponge racquet and walloped that spinning ball into the Stiga's gaping mouth. He hadn't lost his windmill motion, his signature shot.

He showed me the line of equipment—Dick Miles Full Pro balls, nets, and bats—that he'd manufactured once upon a time and sold to Montgomery Ward, J.C. Penny, and K-Mart. He gave me one of his Full Pro racquets, with a "vibration-free sweet spot," where the ideal player dreams of connecting with the ball.

In the 1948 World's at Wembley, he'd played Bo Vana in the quarterfinals, was leading 18-15 in the fifth game. Dick had come from behind to catch up with Vana and take the lead. "That was my Zen experience. I went into a trancelike state." But he lost the match. And Vana reached the finals, where he lost to Bergmann, whom, according to George Weinberg, Miles could "demolish."

"Vana became a fireman," Miles said. That was the fate of ping-pong players, to fall into their own kind of oblivion.

He showed me the *Time* cover (April 26, 1971) that had produced a thunderclap. *China: A Whole New Game*, with Steenhoven & Co. on the Great Wall, the fortifications undulating behind them, and a white banner slashed across the cover's red band: *First Color Photos/Yanks in Peking.*

Miles was almost left out of the picture. "Nobody wanted me in," he said. So he kneeled in front of Steenhoven, and perversely, he was the one who was most prominent—Miles, the American master.

He agreed to hit with me at my hole-in-the-wall on Eighty-sixth Street, Amsterdam Billiards, with its glaring lights and a green felt floor. He was half blind in one eye, had that constant ringing in his ears, and didn't have the breath to play for more than twenty minutes. The glare bothered him . . . and my picot. He kept overshooting the ball.

But he still had the "sizzling chop" that remained in George Weinberg's memory.

I couldn't battle against the Stiga Robot, with its rotating heads, but at least I could do a little damage against Dick Miles.

"Ah," he'd say, "now I can read that shot," and he'd ram the ball right down the middle of the table. "Into the *kishgas* (the Yiddish word for solar plexis) . . . always into the *kishgas*."

"Come," he said. There were too many blind spots at Amsterdam Billiards. We hopped into a cab, rode up to Ninety-ninth and Broadway, and I felt like Alice again, tumbling into unknown territory. But I didn't fall into a hole or go right into the heart of a looking glass. I climbed several flights of stairs to a phantom ping-pong parlor. It had five tables, with a polished wood floor.

"Dick," I asked in my befuddlement, "how long has this place existed?"

"Five, six months."

"But why didn't Marty tell me about it?"

"You know Marty. He won't play unless the conditions are perfect."

It was more than that. This was Dick Miles country, the Manhattan Table Tennis Club, which should never have been there, because New York real estate had jumped over the moon and couldn't afford the luxury of a ping-pong parlor and the space it required. But there was a shrewder, more diabolic, mathematics involved. The club had its very own godfather, a ping-pong aficionado who happened to be a minimogul. He owned the entire building and leased the space to himself. There were no signs out on the street, nothing to declare that this phantom parlor had its own address. It didn't advertise in the *Village Voice* or believe in business cards.

The mogul didn't want duffers coming in off the street. He'd carved out a club for the very best players in New York, had them give him lessons, and allowed them to play for free. He'd defied the laws of economic gravity: if you had your heart's desire, cash didn't have to rain on your head.

I played with Miles under the fluorescent lights. He was reading more and more of my shots. A woman walked in, a refugee from the Balkans, and one of the strongest players at the club; she watched Miles for a couple of minutes and offered to give him lessons.

"I can help you," she said.

Miles laughed. "Help me? I'm seventy-five."

One of the club's regulars handed her a copy of *Table Tennis.* "Sister," he said. "Don't ya know who this is? . . . the Player of the Century."

But she'd never heard of Lawrence's, and the old Broadway culture, where ping-pong had been a vital part of the social fabric, when the Americans were only one step behind the Hungarians and had *nearly* ruled world play.

"Him?" she said, "I could give him ten points any day of the week."

Dick's pride hadn't been piqued. He wasn't trying to score points against this Balkan lady. The Needle might have challenged her on the spot. . . .

We left the club, Miles a trifle slower than me on the stairs. He had a bad valve in his heart. We didn't talk about ping-pong or chess or backgammon.

"Conrad," he said. He was discussing his favorite writer.

"What about Joyce and *Ulysses,* the book you've been reading all your life?"

"*Victory* is the greatest novel that's ever been written."

He'd tried to analyze the novel, learn from it. He decided to note all the time shifts, map them out. He had to stop after twenty pages. He got involved in the fury of Conrad's characters and started to cry. He couldn't violate Conrad with his own little chart.

And I thought to myself: would Samsonov or Waldner or Philou ever have worried about violating Joseph Conrad? Or Lui Guoliang, who loved to read Chinese pulp fiction about sword fights? All the intellect had gone out of the game, the quirky excitement, the anarchic spirit of players who were also underground women and men. And though Miles' new club was above the ground, it had the aura of a basement, with blocked-out windows and the "fluorescent tan" that Reisman loved so much.

Lawrence's had also been aboveground, a leftover speakeasy called the Nutty Club . . . where cellar rats had thrived, along with Dick Miles.

"I'm washed up," he said.

He wasn't talking about ping-pong.

"I can't write anymore. You should have seen me twenty, thirty years ago. Then I could write."

I wouldn't join in his lament. "Cut it out," I said. "And get back to Loving."

He'd read *The Dark Lady from Belorusse,* a memoir I'd written about the Bronx, and had liked the image of a solitary soldier sitting behind an ack-ack gun in the middle of a deserted garden during World War II.

"But Dick," I said, "didn't they have soldiers like that in Central Park?"

"No. I never saw a soldier like that."

He pointed to a building just off Broadway where he'd lived when he was eight. "I have no memories . . . doesn't mean a thing."

"But you could dredge it up. That's what writing is. A dredging operation. Like those guys in metal suits walking around on the ocean floor."

I got onto the subway at Ninety-sixth, and Dick walked back to the apartment house where the Manchurian Candidate could have lived and returned to the dredging operation of his own novel.

TWELVE

Alice and the Unicorn

I WAS THINKING OF HUMPTY Dumpty and the White King and the Unicorn that Alice meets. The Unicorn looks at Alice with disgust.

"What—is—this?"

"This is a child," says one of the White King's messengers.

"I always thought they were fabulous monsters!" says the Unicorn. "Is this true?" Alice's lips curl into a smile. "Do you know, I always thought Unicorns were fabulous monsters, too!"

"Well, now that we *have* seen each other," says the Unicorn, "if you'll believe in me, I'll believe in you."

That best describes the current state of ping-pong in America, a never-never land peopled with unicorns, precocious children, and preposterous kings and queens who rule over nothing at all. Ping-pong is a bit like fencing, an obscure sport whose "hold on the American imagination is minimal," writes Richard Sandomir in the *New York Times*. Ping-pong is warfare, but without padded clothing and wire masks. Cliff Bayer, twenty-three, one of America's hopefuls, who is handsome enough to have appeared in *Esquire* and *Vanity Fair*, couldn't find a single sponsor to send him to the Olympics. The United States Fencing Association had to foot all his bills. But Bayer is the ninth ranked foilsman in the world and was able to beat the world's premier foilist, Sergei Goloubitski of the Ukraine, at a tournament in St. Petersburg. What separates winners from losers, according to Bayer, are those people "willing to rip out their guts on the strip [a long linoleum or cork 'carpet' where the bout takes place] and say, 'This match is mine.'"

American ping-pong has no Cliff Bayer, someone who might possibly beat Samsonov or Lui Guoliang, or even make them shudder a little. Ever since Reisman and Miles, ping-pong in America has been a lost country, mired in the Dark Ages. Marty and Tannehill will blame it on sponge and the new technology, like the Stiga Robot, but that Robot could swallow up Samsonov *and* Lui Guoliang, and why blame sponge and speed glue? The Chinese were actually afraid of Dick Miles at the '59 World's in Dortmund, where Miles, with a "Hock" hard rubber bat, managed to defeat two of China's very best players . . . no, it wasn't sponge, it was America's cultural and psychic isolation that kept ping-pong in the Dark Ages.

Lawrence's had been America's training ground, its "national school" in the heart of Manhattan, and when Herwald Lawrence lost his lease around 1955, ping-pong had nowhere else to go. Lawrence would open a new parlor in the wildlands of upper Manhattan, on 207th Street, but it didn't have the same ambience and aura of the Nutty Club, and the new Lawrence's became one more wasteland. Lawrence returned to midtown as a bookkeeper in the garment district. . . .

He was the first black man to break the color barrier and own an establishment on Broadway, close to Times Square. Though he thrived *after* the era of Legs Diamond and Arnold Rothstein, the first king of organized crime, he could have been a fictional character out of Damon Runyon's *Guys and Dolls* (1931). He was certainly Runyonesque. Born in Barbados, he was six foot three, with hazel eyes, perfectly chiseled features, and a deep melodious voice. There were never any brawls at the club. Lawrence wouldn't have allowed it. And when Lawrence's disappeared, so did ping-pong's nerve center (Reisman's was more of a roost than a training ground). There had been table tennis leagues and intercity play in the thirties and forties, with matches at the old Madison Square Garden, where enthusiasts might watch a Reisman-Miles finale, but all of that has vanished.

Sheri Soderberg Pittman, current president of USATT, envisions a miraculous rebirth, particularly with hard cash pumped in from the United States Olympic Committee. She has even found a perfect slogan, *Pipeline*, whose essence "is to simultaneously widen the base of developing players at the foundation of a triangle-shaped pyramid while generating and supporting elite athletes as they progress to the apex of the triangle" (*Table Tennis*, November/December 1999).

What triangle? Which elite athletes? She could have been talking to Humpty Dumpty. "When I use a word," Humpty says to Alice, "it means just what I choose it to mean—neither more nor less."

Pipeline.

"When I make a word do a lot of work . . . I always pay it extra."

Sheri Pittman sees Olympic and world champion medallists in her dreams. But where will they come from without intercity play and with a single club in Manhattan, run by a little ping-pong pasha?

Adham Shakara, the new president of the ITTF, has even more grandiose schemes. He wants to *market* ping-pong, make it into a profitable enterprise. Having learned to play in Cairo, he emigrated to Canada with his parents when he was still a young boy and was Canadian junior champion in 1969-1970. He attended McGill University in Montreal, graduating as an electronic engineer, and started several businesses. His first order of business as

president of the ITTF was to establish a new office in Lausanne, home of the International Olympic Committee. He was also instrumental in finessing the ITTF Pro Tour, with sixty-five thousand dollars in cash prizes. But the Pro Tour flopped in Fort Lauderdale, and all the king's horses and all the king's men couldn't have put it back together again. Neither Samsonov nor Lui Guoliang could fire the public's imagination, no matter what the prize money.

Shakara has also worked hard for the adoption of the 40mm ball. And like Jean-François Kahn, he believes that the new ball will work its own miracle. "We are being criticized that the ball is not visible on TV. The bigger ball will be more visible, slightly slower and [have] slightly less spin . . ."

But international umpire Paul Kovac doesn't agree. He's one of the few *pongistes* who doesn't live in Humpty Dumpty land. He doubts that the fat ball will increase the popularity of table tennis on TV, "which is the core of the whole campaign. . . . Table tennis is not off the air because the ball flies too fast, and it will not be on the air because the ball flies a little slower." It just can't draw a sufficient audience in the United States. "Table tennis will be put on the list of television's favorite sports when the TV people find [a] sufficient number of sponsors willing to pay 5-7 digit sums for 30 seconds of air time in the hope that the audience will be large, so that they can sell millions of packages of laxatives, rolls of toilet paper and other products." That will never happen, unless Miles and Reisman are reincarnated as Olympic and world champions, or to quote William Butler Yeats, until some "rough beast, its hour come round at last, slouches toward Bethlehem [Pennsylvania] to be born." In other words, it would take a Yankee devil, or AntiChrist, to beat the likes of Lui Guoliang.

But Kovac does have the beginnings of a solution. "The first step in the right direction, at least in this country, would be to organize a successful league." League competition would both sharpen and highlight individual players. "Having a successful league would bring the status of table tennis in this country to a par with that of Europe." I doubt it, unless such a league were strong enough to compete with the Europeans. And that won't arrive for a long, long time.

Larry Hodges, editor of *Table Tennis*, asked Adham Shakara what it would take to bring international tournament play to America. Unlike London, Stockholm, Budapest, Prague, Paris, Cairo, Vienna, Tokyo, Calcutta, Bombay, Sarajevo, Pyongyang, and Kuala Lumpur, no city in the U.S. has ever been the site of a World's.

"…The U.S. would need at least six to eight million in sponsorship to pull it off."

And suppose we found the money? Let's go through the looking glass again and imagine that Bill Gates, the mahatma of Microsoft, is a secret devotee of the sport and offered eight mil with one or two blinks of an eye. Would it matter much? There would still be no real venue for the game. It would be one more nonevent unless a couple of American "killers" suddenly rise up out of nowhere. But they'll never come from Sheri Pittman's *Pipeline*.

I WAS SITTING ON MY BEDROOM floor, pondering the fate of ping-pong. It was a Sunday morning in July. Pete Sampras was playing in the men's final at Wimbledon against Australia's Patrick Rafter. I didn't intend to watch the match, not at nine in the morning. But I had a particular affection for Sampras. I'd watched him win the U.S. Open in 1990, his first Grand Slam. The kid was nineteen. And he played with a *noblesse* that almost wounded me. He was a figure out of Greek tragedy, a hero who lost even

while he won. According to the *New York Times*, Sampras "has no public persona to speak of and is not the celebrity-style athlete of a dot-com age."

Perfect.

To appreciate Sampras, who doesn't have the usual dazzle, "you have to love tennis, understand tennis. He is Hank Aaron, not Babe Ruth. Joe Louis, not Muhammad Ali. Jack Nicklaus, not Tiger Woods."

I wouldn't have made that analogy. He was awesome, overpowering, and didn't have to showboat. On target, utterly concentrated, unlike Joe Louis, who seemed to work out of some deadly dream state, his eyes narrowing as he went in for the kill. Sampras was always wide awake. He suffered from tendinitis in his left shin . . . like a hobbled hero. And I decided to watch him at Wimbledon.

The rain had delayed the match. He lost the first set and was trailing 4-1 in the second-set tiebreaker. The match was slipping away. But Rafter double-faulted and Sampras won the set. It was like watching a pair of Titans duel under the constant threat of rain. Rafter, with his beard and ponytail and "funky good looks," had captured the crowd. But Pete Sampras didn't care.

"We all choke," he said, after his nearly fatal collapse in the first set. "No matter who you are, you just get in the heat of the moment. The title could be won or lost in a matter of shots. I really felt it slipping it away."

And then it was Rafter's turn to choke. Sampras began to grind him down on his way to a record thirteen Grand Slams. And he did it just as "the light was going out. . . . The scene there was unbelievable. It was getting dark, and all those lightbulbs. It was scripted, in a way."

And nothing like that could ever have been scripted in table tennis, even during the classic era. It was Centre Court at Wimbledon, where table tennis really began. Because the game itself grew out of Wimbledon's success, as manufacturers fell all over themselves to find a parlor version of lawn tennis, a little Wimbledon. As Reisman reminded me, there was also an erotic twist. Young, genteel men and women, who had to be chaperoned, could have a kind of subtle courtship . . . without kissing or holding hands. They would bat a ball from opposite sides of a table and look into each other's eyes.

But when lovers could hold hands and kiss without a chaperone, ping-pong lost its erotic edge. It still existed under the shadow of lawn tennis. "Yet," wrote Murray Kempton, "there is a history of ping-pong as there is a history of mankind, marked too by misfortune, regularly interrupted by catastrophe, occasionally redeemed by mystical illumination. . . ."

In 1937 Sol Schiff developed a fingerspin serve (he would flip the ball against his racquet with the help of his thumb) that was so unreadable, it had to be outlawed.

In 1952 an obscure watchmaker, Hiroji Satoh, arrived in Bombay with his sponge bat, which he carried in a special wooden box. According to Dixie Cartland, the other Japanese players were so ashamed of Satoh's victories, they tried to coach his opponents . . . and failed.

"Satoh was driven to sake," writes Dick Miles, "and this abused, apologetic homunculus who had wrecked the game in 10 days was never seen again in international play."

Wreck the game? I don't agree with Dick.

For the past hundred years the ping-pong bat has been a bald piece of wood in search of some kind of covering. Until Satoh, Bernie Hock was the premier batmaker, at least in the United States. All the champions at Lawrence's used a Hock bat, which was handmade, like a precious watch without moveable parts. "He knew just how I wanted it— with the handles loose, no glue," remembers Miles.

A Hock bat could last for years. After 1952 Hock lost his little monopoly to the big sports manufacturers. But Bernie Hock went right on making bats.

Then came speed glue. The ITTF would love to see the glue banned, but first they have to find another means of fixing sponge to a wooden blade. According to Jean-François Kahn, it will happen very soon.

I welcome the 40mm ball, and also the "fatter one," 44mm, which is currently being used at a clinic in Oita, Japan, for brain-injured patients. A pair of neurologists, Tomohiko Sato and Teruaki Mori, have tried "table tennis therapy" on forty-four patients suffering from brain tumors and head injuries. Almost all of them showed improvement after two and a half months. Patients particularly enjoyed "playing rallies." Ping-pong was much more fun than traditional therapy. Even the three patients who did not improve had much more   "brilliance" in their eyes while batting the big fat ball. . . .

WHAT OTHER SPORT HAS TOURNAMENT rankings for boys and girls under ten . . . and up to eighty and over? Pretty soon there will be a ranking for centenarians, which brings me back to the stress test that Doctors Horowitz and Kahn figured I ought to have if I wanted to play in tournaments, against fifteen-year-olds who were practically immortal. When I told my doctor in Manhattan that both a cardiologist (Steve Horowitz) and a sports physician who specialized in ping-pong (Dr. Kahn) had recommended that I have a stress test, he looked at me with an air of incredulity. I had no *obvious* signs of heart disease. A stress test, he said, had a 5 percent chance of showing a "false positive," and I might have to endure an angiogram, which could be quite dangerous.

Why was he discouraging me?

I persisted. And when I showed up at the hospital a week later, in the "heart room," the nurse shaved my chest and applied little suction cups, attached me to a machine that dripped a clear liquid into my veins, and then the cardiologist came in. I told him about my quest.

"I play ping-pong," I said, "in tournaments."

He himself was a squash player. And he wasn't unkind, but if he had to administer a stress test to everyone who seemed as fit as myself, it would bankrupt the system, he said.

And I thought: it's Alice and Humpty all over again . . . and the horse with anklets round his feet.

"But what are they for?" Alice asks the White Knight.

"To guard against the bites of sharks."

I could have been that horse, with phantasmagoric sharks biting all over the place. You couldn't have a stress test in the modern world of medicine until you were dying on your feet.

I climbed aboard a treadmill, walked and walked as the incline steepened, and the doctor smiled, "now it's like being in a seven-mile marathon."

He noticed an irregularity in the electric window I was wired to.

"It could be the vibrations of the machine . . . we'll know more when we run the nuclear."

What nuclear? I was already alarmed. The incline steepened. I could hardly walk in place. Then the nurse sat me in a wheelchair, and an attendant brought me down to the "nuclear," a machine that was like an open coffin with a roof that was slanted above my heart and could roam across my chest. . . .

The nuclear confirmed that there was nothing wrong or irregular about my heartbeat. I could enter as many tournaments as I liked. But for a moment, while I was in the wheelchair, I hummed a little mantra, *Whatever you do, don't get sick, don't get sick, or you'll have to wear an anklet the rest of your life.*

IT'S THE END OF JULY and the Needle takes me on a little journey. Our chauffeur is Magdi, a Coptic Christian, who can trace back his lineage twenty-five hundred years. He was a commodity trader who lost his fortune in the crash of 1987. Born in Cairo, he was a member of Egypt's secret service who was shot when President Anwar el-Sadat was killed in 1981 by a band of fanatics. He still bears enormous scars on his body. He's a great big man with a booming voice and a deep mark on one side of his face. The Needle is giving lessons to Magdi's son, George, a large, round boy of ten or eleven who looks like a little sultan. We ride uptown to a Department of Parks recreation center that actually has a room of ping-pong tables, another hidden cache that Marty neglected to tell me about.

Everybody salutes the Needle when he arrives. He works out with George, who already has a windmill motion that's better than mine.

I sit until the little sultan's arms are numb. Then Magdi takes us to an Egyptian restaurant on Ninth Avenue. We're treated like aristocrats, because Magdi helped the restaurant owner get his green card. It's chick peas and chicken cooked in a clay pot. All of us eat with our fingers. Magdi reminisces while the dishes continue to come. He talks about Farouk, my favorite king, who haunted the newsreels of my childhood and wandered the earth after he was deposed in 1952. I remember pictures of him playing ping-pong in Monaco or Biarritz, wearing a sailor's hat to keep the sun out of his eyes. "King Farouk left Egypt with seven pots of gold dust," Magdi says. "He practically bankrupted the nation."

But I feel like Scheherezade, ready to weave a tale about that fat wanderer. What's a king without a home? The Needle had had an audience with him, had played in one of Farouk's palaces.

"Marty, what was he like?"

"He clapped after one of my best shots . . . and fell asleep."

Magdi takes out a wallet made of the finest alligator skin. It's seventy-five years old and had belonged to his father. The wallet has an incredible sheen, as if it had been parked in some magnificent display window, beyond the ravages of time.

He'd been on the reviewing stand with Sadat when the assassins struck.

"How did they get that close? His own officers and bodyguards must have betrayed him. Was it because of the Peace Process . . . Camp David?"

Magdi smiles . . . like Scheherazade. It's a tale he'd love to tell.

I can imagine half the secret services on the planet in some cabal against Sadat. Can't help myself. I love intrigue.

I watch the little sultan. Will he be the new Needle? The next Dick Miles? Perhaps I've been too hard on Sheri Pittman. Perhaps America's own pluralism, the gift it has to gather so many different tribes, will pull it out of its ping-pong doldrums.

Lawrence's was a miracle, like Montparnasse in the '20s, but "Montparnasse" will never happen again. Lightning is very superstitious and doesn't like to revisit old territories and themes.

But just as Montparnasse thrived on its magnificent café life, with Kiki as its muse, Lawrence's thrived on Manhattan's enchanted, mysterious night. As Luc Sante says in *Low Life* (1991): "The night is the corridor of history, not the history of famous people or great events, but that of the marginal, the ignored, the suppressed, the unacknowledged. . . . In the streets at night, everything kept

hidden comes forth, everyone is subject to the rules of chance, everyone is potentially both murderer and victim. . . . At night, everyone is naked."

New York has lost much of that nakedness. But so what? I'm betting on the little sultan and others like him, whose moms and dads have come from all over the globe to reinvent themselves; some of their offspring, boys and girls, will stumble onto ping-pong . . . perhaps on a rainy afternoon, like Ruth Aarons; at a settlement house, like the Needle; or a grammar school, like Jean François Kahn; or a country orchard, like the picot kid. . . .

THIRTEEN

The Horse Whisperer of Paris

I WAS READING WILLIAM MAXWELL'S obit in the *Times*. A novelist and fiction editor at the *old* New Yorker, he'd worked with Vladimir Nabokov, John Updike, and J.D. Salinger, and died in Manhattan at ninety-one, a native of Illinois. I have no idea if he'd ever played ping-pong. In 1997, nearing ninety, he wrote: "I tell myself that lying down to an afternoon nap that goes on and on through eternity is not something to be concerned about. What spoils this pleasant fancy is the recollection that when people are dead, they don't read books. This I find intolerable."

I had to agree. Books rescued me from oblivion, from the feeling that I was so different, so flawed, I had no right to live among people. How I struggled to gather words in the caves and dunes of the Bronx, where you couldn't find a single book, where libraries existed on another planet. Language, as only Alice and Humpty understood, "is worth a thousand pounds [or dollars] a word."

And when I did stumble upon a library, in some distant dune, and read *The Brothers Karamazov* with the help of Webster's Unabridged, hidden in one of the library's nooks, I started to cry.

"Child," the librarian said, "what on earth is the matter with you?"

"I'm so happy," I said.

How could I have made her understand that Karamazov country was as wild and bleak as the Bronx, and that I was no more crazy than the Karamazovs themselves, who could cry or laugh without any reason and suffer long, long laments.

A thousand pounds a word.

Ping-pong also had a language that was impossible to grasp. It belonged to the wisest of women and men, like Leah Neuberger or Reisman and Miles and my coach, Jean-Louis, who saw my frailties in an instant and led me toward the picot, the one advantage I'd ever have on the table.

I was a city boy who'd discovered ping-pong in a country orchard and had my first lesson with an outlaw, Jeff, the army deserter from Rat Island who'd taken time out from romancing Muriel, the farmer's daughter, because he pitied my condition as Muriel's slave and recognized my own outlaw streak.

I could never have been a money player, like the Needle, but wasn't I also a confidence man, tricking people, blowing wool over their eyes, asking them to take some mystery tour across a jungle of words? I could only write the way Dick Miles had once used his chop. Without a moment of mercy.

I've become the bilateral man, left-brained, right-brained, traveling between two continents, two cities, with my picot and an Olympiette portable, which is no longer manufactured in an era of Microsoft Windows, and costs me a fortune to replace a single key.

I've arrived in the new century with an electronic address: jeromecharyn@aol.com, but I still can't punch out a complete page on my Hewlett Packard Laser Jet. All my files and floppy disks are riddled with viruses. I'm like Robinson Crusoe, marooned in cyberspace.

But I have my racquet. And I teach yet another language, the décor of film, at a phantom university on the avenue Bosquet that's accredited by some mysterious American association and run by equally mysterious French labor laws. I'm a permanent impermanent member of the faculty with a contract *indeterminé*. It sounds like a death sentence . . . or an invitation to some horrible heaven.

I cannot conquer French. I'm the lord of one novel, Flaubert's *L'éducation sentimentale* (which I read line by line with my tutor, Lil), and only confirms my deepest suspicions about life, art, and the novel. Flaubert's hero, Frédéric Moreau, a sleepwalker if I ever saw one, drifts through the novel, in love with a married woman, Madame Arnoux, and not only discovers less and less about his own life, but seems to unravel into a permanent state of nothingness.

He traveled.

He discovered the melancholy of ocean liners, cold awakenings under a tent, the giddiness of landscapes and ruins, the bitterness of interrupted friendships. . .

And all he's left with is "the idleness of his intelligence and the inertia of his heart."

Ah, what a master to have picked! And in a foreign land, no less. Flaubert might have been describing my own giddiness and "unbearable lightness of being."

And perhaps that is why I came to Paris in the first place, to lose my bearings, like a compass robbed of its magnetic pull, so that I would remain a child within the trappings of French culture, relying on nothing more than the debris I'd collected in the caves of the Bronx.

I didn't weep after reading Flaubert. I had no Karamazovs to play against the inertia of my heart. I only had Frédéric, my horrible, wasted twin.

And I suppose that's why I fell in love with ping-pong as a boy. It soothed me. Jeff of Rat Island had his own brand of chivalry with a ping-pong bat.

Just as it soothed me to watch Dick Miles for the first time, at Morris' club in the bowels of the Ansonia. He was arrogant, indifferent to the world as he chopped and chopped. No one could approach him, no one could give him a game . . . the only dialogue he could ever really have was with himself.

And then I'd discovered Jean-Louis Fleury at U.S. Metro, when it was still on Philosophy Street. He had an intelligence with his racquet, a whiplike motion that was light years beyond my comprehension. After he'd started training me, I had to return the gift of time. I bought him a killer's bat, a Mark V with the fattest sponge available and a pot of speed glue, at the little ping-pong boutique, actually a crowded closet, near the place d'Italie.

Jean-Louis had been playing in tournaments against "gluers" and had lost a nanosecond of quickness against them. With the Green Hornet, as I liked to call his new weapon, he regained his edge. I can barely describe the pleasure I got from watching him play against shakehanders or penholders as he whipped or spun with the Green Hornet . . . or when I played against him, in one of our training sessions, and could feel the Hornet's sting, and the whole range of his "language"—because ping-pong was a language and I'm not talking about the weighted down paraphernalia of its rules and terminology. I mean something else: the ineffable music of its motions, the dancelike gestures at the table, the talent of heart and mind that could bend the body to its own will.

I had little of it, perhaps none . . . and perhaps Jean-Louis' skills (and the Needle's, or Dick Miles' and Philou's) were outside language itself and were the dreamlike maneuvers of a superior machine. And language, as Flaubert said in *Madame Bovary*, was like a cracked kettle on which we beat out our silly songs for bears to dance to while we long to move the stars. . . .

And I'm both the singer and the song, a cumbersome black bear with his own kettle, banging to amuse himself . . . and keep the wind out of my pants.

But the greatest fun I've ever had in ping-pong was playing against Frédéric. No, he's not the same character out of *L'éducation sentimentale*. *My* Frédéric is a clown. He acts, does monologues on the radio, and sells bric-a-brac at various flea markets. Everybody despises poor Frédéric. The first time I saw him he got into a fight with Moustaki. He was so boisterous, running, shouting, belching, that Georges could barely occupy his own table. It seemed that Frédéric couldn't survive without two tables—yours and his. He banged into Georges, wouldn't apologize. They eyeballed one another. But Moustaki isn't a brawler, he's a gentleman, an Alexandrian Jew. Still, he was angry, in the heat of a game against Humpty Dumpty (aka Jerome), but after grumbling, Frédéric walked away.

He was only a touch below Jean-Louis' caliber, but he wandered from team to team at our club. He would unsettle every match, destroy the equilibrium of entire clubs. And pretty soon he had to join a league where he was the only player . . . nobody wanted Frédéric.

But he was loyal to U.S. Metro. And one afternoon, arriving with the biggest, fattest training bag that was part of his peculiarity, he whistled, broke wind, and asked me to play.

He was often so funny in his gestures—half-King Kong, half-acrobatic angel—that he would smash right through your defense.

And so I hit some balls with him, had a little warm-up match. He could have spot me ten points. But it wouldn't have been high drama, or much fun for Frédéric, who was as burly and thick as a bear, yet could move with all the thrust of an antelope. A savage attacker, he would turn the tables on me, oblige me to attack as he transformed himself into *Fred le défenseur*. And no matter how hard I hit, or where I placed the ball, he would leap about and come up with it. And whenever he missed, couldn't trap a deeply angled shot, he would curse himself. "Lazy bones. *Feignasse*."

Or if I couldn't read one of his "soft" serves, he would stop and squint at me. "Come on, Jerome. You're playing like a grandma."

We would have incredible volleys, because he took me outside the usual barometer of the game, wasn't trying to annihilate me, to destroy my confidence, but keep the ball in constant motion. But I couldn't stop laughing as Frédéric spun and mimicked his own movements. And if he fell far behind, he would slam the ball into my *kishgas* (as Dick Miles liked to say) and I would have to rely on my picot; that maniac defense would startle him a little. He would bluster and miss an easy shot. But it was my own laughter that undid me. I couldn't resist the clown.

Fred managed to get on the bad side of our president, Jacob. He would arrive late, interrupt some "corpo," a match between players of different corporations, like Thomson or one of the big banks, which had their own leagues. And Jacob, who had warned Frédéric not to interfere, finally banished him from the club.

I remember Frédéric arriving with his enormous bag *after* his banishment. Jacob screamed as Fred started to warm up. Jacob screamed again. Fred had to pack his gear and leave, and I felt like a little boy stranded in a country orchard, helpless and alone.

I wasn't the only one who mourned the big bear. Even Moustaki had grown fond of him. We signed a petition, ten or twelve of us, begging Jacob to give Frédéric one more chance. But Jacob wouldn't budge. He'd resign, he said, if Frédéric entered our little "teapot" on the allée Verte, so we continued to mourn the big bear. . . .

IN THE THICK OF BATTLE with Moustaki one afternoon, I thought about the city where he was born, which lost its European flavor after '52, when Egypt's strongman, Gamal Abdel Nasser, began to kick out the Brits, the French, and the Jews . . . until Alexandria became " a provincial backwater" with broken sidewalks and dark and dirty streets.

It had been the showpiece of Alexander the Great, who founded the city in 332 BC, with a central avenue, the Canopic Way, that connected "the Gate of the Sun at one end . . . to the Gate of the Moon at the other," according to Alexander Stille. It would grow into "the world's first true metropolis," with an "opulent, multicultural . . . population," and a complete babel of tongues. Nothing was foreign to Alexandria. And the heart of this ancient cosmopolitanism was Alexandria's Great Library, with six hundred thousand papyrus scrolls and enough scholars, scientists, and librarians to rival any modern think tank.

These librarians and their masters were also pirates. Ships that docked in Alexandria had to "hand over any manuscript or scroll on board for copying. The Alexandrians then returned the copy and kept the original."

But the library vanished under mysterious circumstances, and with it much of the knowledge of the ancient world. When Richard Nixon came to Alexandria in 1974 and wanted to stand on the library's former site, his Egyptian hosts shrugged their heads. They didn't have a clue where the Great Library had once stood.

Was it in some sand dune, like the Bronx? I envied those lost scholars and librarians who might have invented the prototype of ping-pong in 20 or 30 BC, using swords to bat human skulls across a kitchen table. And I also envied Moustaki, who'd grown up before Nasser's revolution and had his own Great Library in his father's bookshop. . . .

IT'S JUNE 6, AND GEORGES is scheduled to sing at the Olympia, Paris' mythic music hall on the boulevard des Capucines, where Mistinguett and Piaf had once performed, and the great clown Grock. It's a one-night stand for Georges, and the Olympia is sold out. I can't beg or borrow a ticket. But Michel Courteaux, our retired jockey at the club, calls and says that he's found two tickets, a gift from Georges.

I meet him outside the Olympia, with Moustaki's name in enormous red-lit letters on the front wall. We collect our tickets and enter the grand salon, which looks like a giant horseshoe. Elisabeth, Moustaki's original trainer, is at the bar, drinking champagne. She's come to see her pupil, Georges. We hug and do a little dance, like a pair of acrobats at the Olympia. And then Michel and I walk right into the belly of the music hall, with its red carpet and two thousand red chairs. I'm surprised to see how intimate the auditorium feels, like someone's red living room. We sit down. And behind us, scattered in different seats, like a ragtag army, are other refugees from the allée Verte.

"Tout ping-pong," says Michel with a smile.

We talk about the 40mm ball that will be used in local tournament play, come January.

"That fat ball will float right into my pocket . . . . Michel, what if all the officials get wise and ban my picot?"

He tells me not to worry. "The picot has existed before Methuselah. Job played with a picot."

And it's hard to say why Michel moves me so much. Perhaps it's his long silences, the sadness in his face, as if he's always been in mourning. I'm the musketeer of words, curious about one thing: Michel's life as a jockey. I've misinterpreted his silence. Michel does have a language of his own: the language of horses and the men who train them.

Michel is short and very slight, about five-foot-two. The perfect size for a jockey. He hadn't come to horses by any accident. His father had owned an *écurie*, a horse farm and stable, near Bordeaux, and had also been a trainer and a jockey, like Michel. His father had a passion for horses, but none of his sons inherited this passion, except Michel. "J'ai le don pour les animaux . . . fort, tres fort." Michel had the "gift." There was a certain magnetism between Michael and his father's horses. He slept near them. "An animal understands who loves him. He responds to your gestures. He's part of the family. You have to raise him like an infant, nurse him through sickness, operations, and the grippe. You have to care permanently." And that's what Michel did.

He started to train when he was ten and would pass his qualifying exams and become a professional jockey at eighteen. There were no vacation days for Michel. It was now *père et fils*, father and son. He would travel in a large van with five or six horses to race tracks throughout Germany, Switzerland, Italy, Belgium, Sweden, and France.

I asked him if he'd ever taken a bad fall. He rolled his eyes and laughed. "Pas tomber un cheval, c'est un monteur," he said. "La chute est une chute." A fall is a fall. A couple of horses "broke my balls."

But the hardest part wasn't the racing, it was the dressage, the breaking in of a horse, which could be "very dangerous. If the horse doesn't like you, he'll bite you . . . or do worse." Michel would begin to caress and talk to each *poulain*, each colt. He was a whisperer, a man who had talked to horses. "You have to know a horse deeply," he said.

When his father died, Michel sold the farm. "I cried for days." He still hasn't got horses out of his blood . . . or his father's stable. "I think about it often," he said.

I'd found his subject, and he was far more eloquent and passionate than I could ever have been.

We returned to *le ping*. I asked him if he'd lost anything after twenty years of play. "You observe better," he said. "I play better now even if I'm less strong. You can bother your opponent a hell of a lot more."

Unlike me, Michel won most of his matches, this horse whisperer of Paris.

Moustaki came onto the stage in his signature white shirt and pants. The whole Olympia was filled with his fans. We clapped and shouted. Georges' own designs, the little drawings and paintings he liked to do, were projected on the rear wall of the stage. Then images of Bogart and Bergman from *Casablanca*, Gable and Crawford from an early talkie, *Dance, Fools, Dance* (1931), where Gable's a gangster, a bit like Gabin. It was nostalgia night at the Olympia. And Georges did his old favorites, "Le Métèque," "Joseph," "Ma Liberté" . . .

> *J'ai changé de pays*
> *J'a perdu mes amis*
> *Pour gagner ta confiance*
> *Ma liberté . . . **

> (* I've changed countries
> I've lost my friends
> To win your confidence
> My *liberté* . . .)

Georges *owned* the Olympia. It was his private *écurie*.

MICHEL RUNS A LITTLE TOURNAMENT on the allée Verte to celebrate the coming of the 40mm ball. Moustaki can't play. He's singing in Portugal. Michel has us draw lots, so that the pairings will be even: a strong player will team up with a weaker one. I draw Alain, my old training partner from the rue Pascal. We're both *défenseurs*. Which one of us can lead the attack?

We lose our first match, fall back into the consolation part of the tournament. We play against a pair of attackers, but both Alain and I are getting used to the fat ball. We control the tempo, create a lot of mischief for our rivals, and win. We move on to the finals, against a ferocious young attacker and my friend Jean-Claude, a wine merchant.

My picot confuses the young attacker, and Alain defends against the few kill shots he manages to make. We win the consolation prize, a pair of silver trophies that Michel has paid for out of his own pocket.

I've also won my first literary prize, the Liger d'Or, given by the five thousand grade schoolers of Amboise, Bléré, and Château-Renault, in the three valleys of the Loire. The president of the jury, Mr. S., Inspecteur d'Education Nationale d'Amboise, has preselected eight books for the children to choose from. And he's honest enough to tell me that he picked mine, *Bande á part*, about a friendly young giant, Jumbo, and his little band in the worst section in the Bronx, because he wanted to give the pupils a touch of the exotic and a taste of another world. He didn't think it would ever win the Liger d'Or. But the kids of the three valleys adored the tale of Jumbo and his rival giant, Elliott Broken-Head.

Mr. S. picks me up at the railroad station of Saint-Pierre-des-Corps, outside Tours, and drives me to a tiny village near the castle of Clos-Lucé, where Leonardo da Vinci lived out the last years of his life, under the protection of François Premier, king of France.

We arrive at a slightly barren meeting room across the road from the actual schoolhouse. This meeting room is in the middle of a vineyard. I'm intrigued. The *instituteur*, Philippe, has encouraged his students, a band of nine and ten year olds, to sketch my two Bronx giants on the wall. They look like kindly scarecrows, characters who might belong in an orchard. The children are suspicious. One of their other teachers had shown them a picture of me taken right off the Internet. And I don't seem to resemble this man. They think I'm a stand-in, a double of the author, some kind of marionette. The ghost of a ghost.

They ask me questions they have prepared with the help of the *instituteur*.

Where is the Bronx and what is it all about?

What will happen to Elliott Broken-Head? Will he ever get to college?

I answer, searching for a melody I'll never find. "Le Bronx," I say, "le Bronx . . ."

And then I interrogate the interrogators.

"Aimez-vous le tennis de table?" They pretend not to understand my question. I'm only a marionette from Mars.

Then one of the kids takes pity on me. "Le ping-pong," he says.

We leave the vineyard and waltz across the road to the village schoolhouse, which has a ping-pong table in a little open shed. I'm like a big baby. I can't control myself. "Would anybody like to play a little ping?"

Fool that I am, I forgot to bring my picot.

The *instituteur* volunteers to play. He hands me a balding sponge racquet. He's an athlete. I can tell that from his very first strokes. We warm up, and he wallops me right off the table. I smile at him and curse under my breath. *Never, never go anywhere without your picot.*

The kids ask me for my autograph, even if I am only a marionette.

And on the train, coming back from Tours, with the trophy in my hand, a gold-painted statuette, I think of the curious arc of my own life, from that first ping-pong match in the orchard to my defeat in the village near Leonardo's last home. I'm a *pongiste*, that's all. It's my cocaine and my honeydew. I can keep *L'éducation sentimentale* inside my head, with *Citizen Kane* and *Pulp Fiction*, and certain erotic moments, like Muriel and the tank top she forgot to wear, and still plot my next match. Will it be against a cocky kid who'll look at me with contempt? The horse whisperer, who can chew up my picot? Poor forgotten Frédéric, whom our president, the good Jacob, will pardon, like a gift from God? I fashion words. Fine. I hunt in the wildlands, the white spaces between each sentence. But I wouldn't be much of a hunter without my picot. Mock me, kill me. I am who I am.

Postscript: Milan. . .and Michael French

HISTORY TURNS AND TURNS IN funny ways. The past creeps into the future, leaving us with a false present tense, as if every single one of us is wearing a mask. I was leafing through an old issue of *France Tennis de Table* (September 1998), when I fell upon an article entitled "Michel Glikman Cet Inconnu" (Glikman, the Unknown Man), and that name slapped at me like a troubling dream. I'd heard of Michel Glikman, had even written about him. He'd toured with Ruth Aarons, was her exhibition partner, under the "mask" of Michael French. But I wasn't lucky with "Michel Glikman Cet Inconnu." Most of the article had been ripped out of the magazine. I only had the first page. It talked about Michel's odyssey from Dvinsk to Riga and Paris. He was born Mykolas Glikmanos in 1909, the son of a Lithuanian national. His family moved to Paris while Mykolas was still in his teens, and he was "reborn" as Michel Glikman. His older brother opened a radio factory that flourished until the war, and Michel, who was already Lithuania's ping-pong champion, continued to "flirt" with the little white ball.

That's as far as his odyssey went on one page. But in the upper right corner was the photograph of a young man with a moustache, a racquet in his left hand. I assumed this was Michel. Another southpaw, like me.

I scribbled a note to *France Tennis de Table*. Was Glikman, who had to be in his nineties now, still alive? And could the magazine send me a copy of the whole article? Glikman was indeed alive, in Neuilly. I even had his telephone number and the missing pages of the article. I was a bit let down. My mystery man with the moustache wasn't Michael Glikman. The photograph reached across a second page and revealed *another* guy. He was tall and incredibly handsome, like young Robert De Niro in *Godfather II*. He had both hands behind his back, and I couldn't tell if he was a southpaw or not. There was also a much larger portrait of Michel at some boîte with a balcony, the site of France's 1931 nationals, where Michel was crowned the new king. But he didn't wear that crown very long. Raymond Verger, the former champion, bullied the FFTT into passing a law that said only men and women with French nationality could play in the championships. And Michel was one more métèque, with a Lithuanian passport.

His ping-pong club on the rue Marbeuf was filled with émigrés—Hungarians and Czechs who could destroy most of the French players. In 1934 Michel traveled to the United States on the *Ile-de-France*, where he met Jascha Heifetz, the most celebrated violinist of his era . . . and a ping-pong addict, according to the article.

He also met Ruth Aarons, and after she was world champion he would appear with her at the Rainbow Room, with Ginger Rogers and Fred Astaire in the audience. Ping-pong had become the rage all of a sudden. Rogers and Astaire could dance at either end of a ping-pong table as wickedly as they could on a polished studio floor. Harpo Marx and Danny Kaye were *pongistes* who had their own little Hollywood league.

Homesick, "Michael French" returned to France. He became a chauffeur attached to the ministry of health. Soon he was caught in the maelstrom of World War II. He had to wear yet another mask. He hid out in Lyon, assumed the identity of a certain "Jacques Alfandari," a repatriated prisoner of war. With his false papers, he could sit in cafés, assume some kind of normal life. He joined the Resistance, and when the "Ricains" arrived in Lyon, he found himself an interpreter for the American army. In 1945 he became a naturalized citizen of France . . . .

That's where the article stopped. There was nothing more about Michel Glikman the *pongiste*. I called him in Neuilly. "Ruth Aarons," I said. I must have sounded like some curious vulture out of his past. But Michel agreed to meet with his American admirer. I took the Metro to Neuilly-sur-Seine, marched across the place Winston Churchill, and arrived at the rue Borghése, a little street of garden apartments, where Michel lived with his wife Yolande, a youngster of eighty-six.

He was a bit stooped, but he had the halting dance of a ping-pong player. I wanted to get past the formalities of an interview. We were landsman, after all, wanderers who'd come to France by some twist of fate.

"What's a nice Jewish boy from Lithuania doing in Neuilly?"

He laughed and started to tell me about Ruth Aarons and Jascha Heifetz. He hadn't met Heifetz aboard the *Ile-de-France*. It was Heifetz's secretary, who introduced him to the *master* after they landed in New York.

"Was he a good ping-pong player?"

"No," Michel said, "but he tried. . ."

Michel was staying with relatives in Reading, Pennsylvania. "I had nothing to do. They didn't take me seriously . . . I was a ping-pong player."

"But why didn't you get some kind of job?" Michel couldn't remember. But he did remember coming into Manhattan by bus. He joined a ping-pong club on Broadway.

"Was it Lawrence's?"

The name meant nothing to him. "It was on the second floor," he said. He found his New York Table Tennis Association membership card for the season of 1934-35. The association's address was 1721 Broadway. I smiled at my little bit of detection: 1721 Broadway was also Lawrence's address.

I asked him about the other *pongistes* at Lawrence's.

"There was no American who played as well as me."

Michel and Hungarian Sandor Glanz dominated the field. Unlike the locals at Lawrence's, Michel had already played at the World's in Berlin, Budapest, and Prague, as part of the Lithuanian team.

"I wasn't the best player," he said, "but the most spectacular." And an article in the *Allentown Chronicle* of June 18, 1935, described the particulars of Michel's game. "His remarkable long reach gives him an advantage over most of his opponents. Playing fifteen to twenty feet back, he picks up the ball before it hits the floor, returning it with an ace-like velocity."

But it was at Lawrence's where he discovered Ruth Aarons, or where Ruth Aarons discovered him. He encouraged her to play at the next World's, in Prague, where she would win the women's singles. . . with the help of Sandor Glanz and Michel Glikman.

In 1937 he got a letter from Ruth, inviting him to take part in her floor show. He joined her in London, where she baptized him "Michael French." He went back with Ruth to America on a whirlwind tour of ten states. Michael French tantalized the women in the audience. He was a noted ladykiller, a *tombeur*. He met Ginger Rogers at the Rainbow Room, dazzled her. "She wanted to take me back to Hollywood. I didn't go . . . it wasn't serious."

"What about Ruth Aarons?" I asked.

"She was a kid. And she was always chaperoned. Her mother and brother were always with us in the same car. Her brother was our manager and the referee during our matches."

"Could she beat you?"

"Never. Ruth Aarons couldn't beat a man. I made her win many times. We were very popular. I had visiting cards printed with the name 'Michael French.'"

His trips to America had *seasoned* Michel, given him a sense of the New World. As he told the *Allentown Chronicle* in 1935, "the country was one vast landscape, unbroken, as Europe's landscape is, by boundary lines and strong national spirit."

This strong national spirit would soon career crazily into war. But Michel couldn't stay in America. "I didn't like American women."

"Why not?"

"They were always drinking beer . . . I was foolish at that time."

And he fell right back into Europe's maw and murderous boundary lines. He ended up in Lyon during the Occupation, protected by his false papers and his good looks. And one afternoon, while he was at a bar, someone tapped him on the shoulder. Michel was convinced it was the Gestapo. "I turned white like paper." But it was his boyhood friend, Henri Borosh, with whom he'd played soccer in Paris. Borosh had come by plane from London, where Winston Churchill had encouraged him to organize an underground network. "Jacques Alfandari," aka Michel Glikman, aka Michael French, immediately became part of the Borosh network.

His father and two brothers were in a detention camp outside Lyon. Michel bribed a local policeman to get them out of the camp. For three years his father and brothers hid in Lyon, never leaving their apartment . . . .

Did Michel pick up ping-pong after the war? He never played with another club. He was a lost ping-pong player, a *pongiste perdu*. But I was fascinated by the photographs in *France Tennis de Table*. A certain Count Fernand Palmiéri had been president of the FFTT from 1929 to 1933. And Michel's own peregrinations had brought me much closer to French ping-pong, which wasn't part of my own personal history. I asked him about that villain, Raymond Verger, who'd blackballed him from the national championships.

"It was jealousy," Michel said. "The other people were a hundred percent for me . . . he didn't like it that I was Jewish."

The ex-*pongiste* began working for an American millionaire, carted him around in a Rolls Royce. And when the millionaire retired, he gave the Rolls to Michel, who would become his own liveryman until he was eight-six. "When I was eighty I looked seventy . . . no one wants to have a driver who's eighty years old." Michel was quite generous with his memorabilia. He gave me a photograph of Ruth Aarons, himself (with the racquet in his right hand, alas), his Rolls, and a card advertising his act with Ruth at London's May Fair Hotel. . . .

He didn't want anything back. I'd become the keeper of Michel's own strange vagabondage. His wife drove me to the Metro in her own small car. "Sorry," she said. "It's not the Rolls." She was born in Paris during the "Great War." Her earliest memories were of hiding in a cellar while the German cannons—Big Berthas—shelled the town.

"Big Bertha," I muttered and got out of the car.

THE UNKNOWN, UNCELEBRATED MICHEL GLIKMAN had suddenly turned French ping-pong into a familiar family. I'd listen to the "veterans" at U.S. Metro talk about their own favorites: Michael Haguenauer, Guy Amouretti, and Jacques Secrétin. Haguenauer ruled French ping-pong as a singles and doubles champion from 1933 to 1959. Amouretti, who flourished during the same era, was French singles champion seven times. The photo I have of Guy reveals a sad-eyed man with a moustache. He and Haguenauer grew up in the golden age of pong, before sponge. Jacques Secrétin, born in 1949, was France's first great sponger (he won the singles seventeen times), and its most visible champion . . . until Philou. I'd arrived in Paris during "Philou fever" and quickly developed my own form of amnesia about France's ping-pong past. But I should have remembered Secrétin. I'd encountered him at the Gentlemen's in 1994. He was one of the "clowns" who performed after Patrick Chila and Philou. He'd also demolished Tim Boggan, George Brathwaite, and Jack Howard in a televised match, when those three American musketeers had come to France in 1971, in the wake of Ping-Pong Diplomacy.

And now there was a new fever. The Olympics. Jean-François Kahn had promised to take me to INSEP, France's school for champions in the bois de Vincennes, but the coaches were too involved with training the Four Musketeers and Anne Boileau (France's top female player), all of whom had qualified for the summer games in Sydney. And I had to wait.

Meanwhile, Philou and Patrick Chila brought home a medal (bronze) in the men's doubles, defeating Lee-Chul-seung and Yoo Seung-min of South Korea.

I had lunch with Dr. Kahn at a restaurant near Pitié-Salpêtrière. I told him Dr. Horowitz's thoughts about aging and *le ping*, how many of Steve's own heart patients had given up exercise, how ping-pong had revitalized some of them and had helped fight depression. Dr. Kahn smiled, but he wouldn't concede.

"It's difficult to know who's in danger. Ping-pong's not like playing cards." He repeated what he'd said at La Coupole: ten to twelve people died each year at the table.

"In the world?" I asked.

"In France."

He wasn't against the *idea* of training; it was competition that troubled him. "As you get older, the performance of the heart decreases. During competition there's an increase of blood pressure . . . sometimes it's enough to cause an 'accident.' It's a question of chance."

But how could I continue to train in a club where everyone else was a gladiator? If I were a bit less serious, I would lose. I wasn't Ponce de Lion, I insisted, looking for a mystical fountain.

"I can't decide for you," he said. "I can't tell you not to play."

I'd already slowed down, I said. I was on the weakest team, where each match didn't matter so much. But if I gave up the *pleasure* of competition, I'd have to retreat into some corner reserved for discards and *débiles*. I was willing to take the risk.

"Now we enter into problems that are metaphysical," he said, with that same sweet smile.

"It's a mystery. One of our players is dying. Six months ago he was wiping me off the table. I don't understand."

"You're not the only one who doesn't understand. Medicine is an art . . . and a mystery."

We took the Metro and a bus to the bois de Vincennes and arrived at INSEP. It looked like a sanitarium in the middle of the woods. Thomas Mann's magic mountain . . . minus the mountain.

There were guards at the front gate, and Dr. Kahn had to show some kind of ID. But he was recognized at once as an "insider," someone who'd worked within these walls for three years, attending to gifted young athletes who trained and often lived at INSEP. I was allowed into the complex with Dr. Kahn, though I felt invisible among this little nation of athletes and their keepers.

We strolled across the grounds. It was odd to see a hairdresser's at INSEP, a beauty salon. But why shouldn't athletes in the bois de Vincennes have their own *coiffure?* We passed a biomechanics lab, which stressed "Movement, Action, and Performance." We passed an indoor stadium and a laboratory devoted to the different aspects of gymnasium floor coverings and got to the Centre Sportif Jean Letessier, named after a boxing champion. It was the only modern building I'd discovered in the entire compound. It was a series of enormous wooden cubes, each one resting *dangerously* on top of the other, so that the Centre Sportif seemed about to tilt . . . like Humpty Dumpty. But there was a more pressing problem. The wood had begun to warp.

"It's the rain," said Dr. Kahn.

But this very warping had given the Centre Sportif a rustic feel in INSEP's world of brown brick. I saw archers and boxers in the basement. We climbed a flight of stairs. The inside of the building was like a crooked aircraft hangar.

Milan Stencel, INSEP's head ping-pong coach, had invited us to catch a glimpse of the next generation of champions, sitting on a bench with pots of glue. I recognized Michel Martinez and Sandrine Morel, two of France's young stars.

The women players had a more difficult time than the men. They couldn't make a career of ping-pong, earn the same money as Philou or Patrick Chila from sports equipment contracts. Most of them left at an early age. There were less than ten women in the training room and over twenty men. They were all gluing like mad. It was the Hungarians, according to Dr. Kahn, who "invented" speed glue in the 1980s. And like Satoh's sponge racquet, speed glue quickly traveled across the globe and turned ping-pong into even more of an offensive game.

The men and women warmed up on opposite sides of the room. They swung their hips, stretched like giraffes. Meanwhile, Dr. Kahn told me about Milan Stencel, who was from Croatia, and had been the national coach of Holland, Belgium, and Italy. He'd come to INSEP in 1997. He had the reputation of being very tough. Dr. Kahn remembered hearing him shout at his players during a match, when Milan was still the Belgian coach.

I expected to meet some kind of monster with a bull neck, but I liked him instantly when he strode into the room. He had the aura of a man who was comfortable inside his own skin. He could have been a character out of my own childhood, a Central European pirate caught in the Bronx . . . one more métèque, like Moustaki, Michael French, and me.

We went up to the balcony and watched the players practice. Standing above them, I could have been the eye of a camera. The players would often grunt as they attacked the ball with hypnotic speed. Martinez was tall and lanky, and unlike the others, he would rarely grunt. I could already imagine him as a fifth Musketeer.

Both the men and the women were using the 40mm ball, required for national and international competition since October first. I asked one of the players how he'd adjusted to the heavier ball.

"Simple," he said. "I have a speedier racquet."

We mortals at U.S. Metro wouldn't have to switch until January. But I picked up a "Tibhar 40mm BASIC" and stuffed it into my pocket, like a bad little boy. Had to prepare myself for January, didn't I?

Milan finally had a bit of time to talk. He had a gentle manner for such a bull-necked man.

He mentioned the Musketeers, "those four guys," who were among the top twenty in the world. "There's such a case in all sports, when you have four guys like that. After them there's a big *trou* [hole] . . . it's like a wall, difficult to break."

"What about Martinez?" I asked. "Couldn't he break through the wall?"

But Martinez had "a constitutional injury. He's only practicing once a day," while the others managed to squeeze in a few more hours.

Milan had to find the right balance for his young wizards between practice and school . . . and school seemed to be getting in the way. "Practice is more difficult to make when it's combined with school." The wizards were in school until eleven, then had to be back at school between two and half past four. Milan had to work around this schedule. But he needed more and more time to turn these young wizards into musketeers.

"That's why the French Federation is paying me."

I teased him. "Milan, what's your magic formula?"

He smiled like some Mafia don. "Practice and praying . . ." Then he shouted some instructions to Martinez.

"I have to be harder on the players. In France everything is polite."

Milan had been abroad thirty years, the voyager, the wandering coach. And now the sheriff of ping-pong had come to France. And a forest at the edge of Paris was his new domain.

"It's the national sport in France."

"Ping-pong?"

"No. Politeness. If you want to steal something, you say, 'Sorry, I have to take this away.'"

Milan winked at me and returned to his young wizards. And I left that building of wooden cubes with a big fat stolen ball in my pocket.

Selected Bibliography

Ambrose, Stephen E. *Nixon, Volume Two. The Triumph of a Politician 1962-1972*. New York: Simon and Schuster, 1989.

Boggan, Tim. *Ping-Pong Oddity*. USA Table Tennis, *1999*.

—. "Grand Tour." *USA Table Tennis*, 2000.

—. "Bernie Hock." *USA Table Tennis/Hall of Fame*, 1999.

—. "Herwald Lawrence." *USA Table Tennis/Hall of Fame*, 1999.

—. "Dick Miles–Part I." *USA Table Tennis/Hall of Fame*, 1999.

—. "Dick Miles–Part II." *USA Table Tennis/Hall of Fame*, 2000.

—. "Marty Reisman–Part I." *USA Table Tennis/Hall of Fame*, 1999.

—. "China Revisited." *Table Tennis Topics*, May/June, 1979.

—. "Leah ('Miss Ping') Neuberger." *USA Table Tennis/Hall of Fame*, 2000.

Brooks, Louise. *Lulu in Hollywood*. New York: Alfred A. Knopf, 1982.

Brownmiller, Susan. "Ping-Pong Madness," *Village Voice*, September 28, 1999.

Carroll, Lewis. *Alice's Adventures in Wonderland* and *Through the Looking–Glass*. London: Puffin Books, 1962.

Coren, Stanley. *The Left-Hander Syndrome: The Causes and Consequences of Left-Handedness*. New York: The Free Press, 1982.

Devys, Jean. "Michel Glikman Cet Inconnu." *Tennis de Table*, FFTT (Federation Française de Tennis de Table, hereafter referred to as FFTT), September 1998.

Gurney, Gerald N. *Table Tennis, The Early Years*. East Sussex: International Table Tennis Federation (no date).

Hampton, Wilborn. "William Maxwell, 91, Dies; Author and Legendary Editor," *New York Times*, August 1, 2000.

Hershey, Dave. "The Aristocrat of Hustle." *Sunday News Magazine*, March 18, 1979.

Hoey, Charles. "Evolution of the Table Tennis Hard Bat." *Classic Hardbat News*, December, 1998.

Jacobson, Howard. "Like a Bat Out of Hell." *The Independent*, June 9, 2000.

Kanfer, Stefan, "The Demonic Game of Plock-Plack." *New York Times Magazine*, April 2, 1972.

Kempton, Murray. "Sports." *Esquire*, August 1972.

Kennedy, Ray. "A Little Night Music." *Sports Illustrated*, November 21, 1977.

Kennedy, William. *Legs*. New York: Penguin Books, 1983.

Lo Brutto, Vincent. *Stanley Kubrick*. New York: Da Capo Press, 1999.

Miles, Dick. "Spongers Seldom Chisel." *Sports Illustrated*, November 1965.

—. "A Bat about Ping-Pong." Sports Illustrated, October 1966.

Miller, Henry. *My Life and Times*. Chicago: Playboy Press, 1971.

Nixon, Richard. *The Memoirs of Richard Nixon*. New York: Touchstone Books, Simon and Schuster, 1978, 1990.

Reisman, Marty. *The Money Player*. New York: William Morrow, 1974.

Remnick, David. "Into the Clear: Philip Roth Puts Turbulence in Its Place." *The New Yorker*, May 8, 2000.

Rhoden, William C. "Momentous Victory, Most Nobly Achieved." *New York Time*, July 10, 2000.

Ross, Lillian. *Ernest Hemingway*. New York: Simon and Schuster, 1961.

Sandomir, Richard. "Hoping to Face the Champ Again." *New York Times*, July 12, 2000.

Sante, Luc. *Low Life*. New York: Vintage, 1992.

Shaw, Peter. "A Man Who Made His Mark." *West Side Literary Review*, September 26, 1974.

Stille, Alexander. "Resurrecting Alexandria." *The New Yorker*, May 8, 2000.

Tennis de Table. FFTT, February 1999.

—. FFTT, March 1999.

—. FFTT, May 1999.

—. FFTT, February 2000.

—. FFTT, April 2000.

Turan, Kenneth. "Table Tennis in Microcosm." *Washington Post*, April 16, 1972.

USA Table Tennis Magazine, November/December 1999.

Index